Criminal Justice Responses to Domestic Abuse in Northern Ireland

This book provides a detailed exploration of the responses of the criminal justice system to domestic abuse in Northern Ireland.

The book's primary focus is on developments which have taken place since around 2010, and in particular since the restoration of the Northern Ireland Assembly in January 2020 after a three-year suspension. The book includes discussion of the increased levels of domestic abuse in Northern Ireland in the context of the COVID-19 pandemic and analyses the ways in which the criminal justice system responded. In addition, the book includes in-depth discussion of the Domestic Abuse and Civil Proceedings Act (Northern Ireland) 2021, which had the effect of criminalising coercive control, and the implications of this legislation for Northern Ireland's response to domestic abuse.

The book will be of great interest to academics and researchers from a wide variety of disciplines, such as criminal law, criminology, social policy, human rights, family law, gender studies and sociology, as well as practitioners and those in the voluntary sector who are working in the area of combating domestic abuse. It can also be used on courses at both undergraduate and postgraduate levels which incorporate the topic of domestic abuse.

Ronagh J.A. McQuigg is Senior Lecturer in the School of Law, Queen's University Belfast. Her research interests are in the area of international human rights law, with a particular focus on domestic abuse as a human rights issue.

Directions and Developments in Criminal Justice and Law
https://www.routledge.com/Directions-and-Developments-in-Criminal-Justice-and-Law/book-series/DDCJL

The ways in which crime is constructed in society is of time-honored interest to criminologists across the globe. The ever-changing landscape of what is criminal and what is not affects scholars and policymakers in their approach to the body of law defining prohibited conduct, how that law evolves, and the modes by which it is administered. Rule of law cannot exist without a transparent legal system, strong enforcement structures, and an independent judiciary to protect against the arbitrary use of power. Critical consideration of the mechanisms through which societies attempt to make the rule of law a reality is essential to understanding and developing effectual criminal justice systems. The *Directions and Developments in Criminal Justice and Law* series offers the best research on criminal justice and law around the world, offering original insights on a broadly defined range of socio-legal topics in law, criminal procedure, courts, justice, legislation, and jurisprudence. With an eye toward using innovative and advanced methodologies, series monographs offer solid social science scholarship illuminating issues and trends in law, crime, and justice. Books in this series will appeal to criminologists, sociologists, and other social scientists, as well as policymakers, legal researchers, and practitioners.

1. **Criminal Law and Precrime**
   Legal Studies in Canadian Punishment and Surveillance in Anticipation of Criminal Guilt
   Richard Jochelson, James Gacek, Lauren Menzie, and Kirsten Kramar

2. **Manufacturing Crime**
   The Market's Role in Crime Control
   John Brent and Peter Kraska

3. **The Evolving Role of the Public Prosecutor**
   Challenges and Innovations
   Edited by Victoria Colvin and Philip Stenning

4. **Powers of The Prosecutor in Criminal Investigation**
   A Comparative Perspective
   Karolina Kremens

5. **Beyond Transitional Justice**
   Transformative Justice and the State of the Field (or non-field)
   Edited by Matthew Evans

6. **The Social and Legal Regulation of Domestic Violence in The Kesarwani Community**
   Kolkata, India, and Beyond
   Amrita Mukhopadhyay

7. **Biosecurity, Economic Collapse, the State to Come**
   Political Power in the Pandemic and Beyond
   Christos Boukalas

8. **Black Iconography and Colonial (re)production at the ICC**
   (IN)DEPENDENCE CHA CHA CHA?
   Mwangi Wanjiru

9. **Criminal Justice Responses to Domestic Abuse in Northern Ireland**
   Ronagh J.A. McQuigg

Criminal Justice Responses to Domestic Abuse in Northern Ireland

Ronagh J.A. McQuigg

Routledge
Taylor & Francis Group
LONDON AND NEW YORK

First published 2023
by Routledge
4 Park Square, Milton Park, Abingdon, Oxon OX14 4RN

and by Routledge
605 Third Avenue, New York, NY 10158

Routledge is an imprint of the Taylor & Francis Group, an informa business

British Library Cataloguing-in-Publication Data
A catalogue record for this book is available from the British Library

Library of Congress Cataloging-in-Publication Data
A catalog record has been requested for this book

ISBN: 978-1-032-19965-8 (hbk)
ISBN: 978-1-032-19985-6 (pbk)
ISBN: 978-1-003-26165-0 (ebk)

DOI: 10.4324/9781003261650

Typeset in Times New Roman
by Newgen Publishing UK

Contents

1 Introduction

Domestic abuse affects vast numbers of people throughout all nations of the world, and is an issue which has recently been brought even more clearly into focus, given that levels of such abuse have increased substantially around the globe since the onset on the COVID-19 pandemic.[1] Much has been written regarding domestic abuse; however, there is a scarcity of academic literature which focuses on responses to domestic abuse specifically in Northern Ireland. This jurisdiction has had a troubled past, and studies of violence relating to Northern Ireland have largely focused on the political violence which is part of the history of this jurisdiction. However, it must not be forgotten that throughout the 'Troubles' and indeed in the present day, many people in Northern Ireland have experienced and are indeed still suffering from violence within their own homes. This book aims to address this gap in the literature by providing a detailed and up-to-date case study from an academic perspective of criminal justice responses to domestic abuse in Northern Ireland.

The 'Troubles' undoubtedly impacted upon responses to domestic abuse in this jurisdiction. For example, the primary focus of the police was on addressing the widespread political violence, and issues such as domestic abuse therefore received little attention.[2] However, the focus of the book is on analysing much more recent responses of the criminal justice system to domestic abuse, specifically from around 2010 onwards. In particular, the book seeks to provide commentary on recent and topical issues, and focuses strongly on developments following the restoration of the Northern Ireland Assembly in January 2020 after a three-year suspension. Soon after this date, Northern Ireland, along with the rest of the world, found itself in the midst of the COVID-19 pandemic. Rates of domestic abuse rose substantially, given that the lockdown measures which were adopted, although necessary to limit the spread of the virus, nevertheless resulted in those living in abusive

DOI: 10.4324/9781003261650-1

relationships finding themselves to be even more isolated and trapped in such situations.[3] In addition, the widespread anxiety created by the pandemic in terms of health concerns and also financial worries increased tensions within many relationships, all too often resulting in violence. The book includes discussion of the increased levels of domestic abuse in Northern Ireland in the context of COVID-19 and of the ways in which the criminal justice system responded.

In addition, a specific offence of domestic abuse was introduced in Northern Ireland in March 2021 under section 1 of the Domestic Abuse and Civil Proceedings Act (Northern Ireland) 2021. The new legislation has the effect of criminalising coercive and controlling behaviour, thereby bringing Northern Ireland into line with the other jurisdictions within the UK and Ireland, and also with relevant human rights standards in this regard. The 2021 Act represents a crucial development in Northern Ireland's response to domestic abuse. Being the final jurisdiction within the UK and Ireland to criminalise such behaviour has enabled Northern Ireland's approach to be informed by the legislation enacted in the other jurisdictions and, in some respects, has allowed Northern Ireland to 'cherry-pick' the best aspects of their approaches. However, there are also aspects of Northern Ireland's domestic abuse offence which differ from the approaches of the other jurisdictions. The book seeks to provide in-depth discussion of the new offence and its implications for Northern Ireland's response to domestic abuse.

However, although the enactment of the domestic abuse offence is certainly a very positive development, this will not constitute a panacea to the problem of domestic abuse in Northern Ireland. Legislation in itself is insufficient as regards addressing domestic abuse, and further sustained efforts are necessary to improve the responses of the criminal justice system in Northern Ireland to this issue. In addition, although the criminal justice system plays an important role in addressing domestic abuse, providing an effective response requires a holistic approach involving other aspects such as the provision of sufficient social support measures for victims.

Chapter Outline

Chapter 2 will seek to explore the elements which are needed in order to provide an effective criminal justice response to domestic abuse. In order to do this, the chapter will draw from academic literature and also from relevant human rights standards at the UN level and from the Council of Europe. The chapter will focus on legislative responses as well as the roles played by three key constituent parts of the criminal justice system – the police, the prosecution service and the courts.

At the UN level, the statements which have been made by entities such as Special Rapporteur on violence against women, its causes and consequences, and the Committee on the Elimination of Discrimination Against Women (CEDAW Committee) will be discussed. In relation to the Council of Europe, the Convention on Preventing and Combating Violence Against Women and Domestic Violence (Istanbul Convention) contains provisions which set out standards regarding effective criminal justice responses to domestic abuse. Although the UK has not ratified this instrument to date and is not therefore yet bound by its provisions, the UK is nevertheless a signatory to the Convention, thus demonstrating its intention to become a party at a later date. Also, domestic abuse can constitute a breach of Articles 2,[4] 3,[5] 8[6] and 14[7] of the European Convention on Human Rights (ECHR), and the European Court of Human Rights (ECtHR) has now developed a substantial body of jurisprudence on the question of how criminal justice systems should respond to this issue.[8] Of recent note, in June 2021 the Grand Chamber of the ECtHR issued a judgment in the case of *Kurt v Austria*[9] which focused in particular on police responses to domestic abuse.

Chapter 3 will then proceed to analyse the responses of the criminal justice system in Northern Ireland to domestic abuse prior to 2020. Political violence was a part of life in Northern Ireland for around 30 years from the late 1960s until the late 1990s, and the 'Troubles' certainly impacted upon responses to domestic abuse. However, the focus of the chapter will be on analysing much more recent responses of the criminal justice system to domestic abuse, specifically during the decade from around 2010 until 2019. During this decade, several reports were issued by Criminal Justice Inspection Northern Ireland (CJINI) which focused on the responses of the criminal justice system to domestic abuse,[10] and these reports will be discussed in this chapter. In 2016 the Department of Justice carried out a public consultation on domestic abuse which included the question of whether a specific offence capturing coercive and controlling behaviour should be enacted, and also encompassed the issue of whether a domestic violence disclosure scheme should be developed and implemented in Northern Ireland.[11] The subsequent introduction in 2018 of the Domestic Violence and Abuse Disclosure Scheme constituted an important development which will be examined in this chapter.

Chapter 4 will be devoted to analysing the responses of the criminal justice system in Northern Ireland to domestic abuse during the period from the beginning of 2020 until the elections to the Northern Ireland

Assembly[12] on 5 May 2022. The Assembly was restored in January 2020 after a three-year hiatus, and from March 2020 rates of domestic abuse in Northern Ireland began to rise significantly in the context of the lockdown measures which were adopted as a response to the COVID-19 pandemic. The chapter will include detailed discussion of these increased levels of domestic abuse and will examine the ways in which the criminal justice system responded.

In addition, crucially a specific offence of domestic abuse was introduced in Northern Ireland in March 2021 under section 1 of the Domestic Abuse and Civil Proceedings Act (Northern Ireland) 2021. The new legislation has the effect of criminalising coercive and controlling behaviour, thereby bringing Northern Ireland into line with the other jurisdictions within the UK and Ireland in this regard, and also with relevant human rights standards as regards legislative responses to domestic abuse, as will be set out in Chapter 2. Chapter 4 will include detailed discussion of the new offence and its implications for Northern Ireland's response to domestic abuse.

It has been found that most stalking offences are committed by abusive ex-partners,[13] and in April 2022 legislation on stalking was enacted in Northern Ireland. The Protection from Stalking Act (Northern Ireland) 2022 contains provisions to give effect to the introduction of a new specific offence of stalking and to stalking protection orders, as will also be discussed in Chapter 4. In addition, the chapter will examine the new offence of non-fatal strangulation or asphyxiation which was introduced under section 28 of the Justice (Sexual Offences and Trafficking Victims) Act (Northern Ireland) 2022, also enacted in April 2022; and the ongoing work on the creation of Domestic Abuse Protection Notices and Orders. Also, in December 2020 domestic homicide reviews were introduced in Northern Ireland.

Chapter 5 will summarise the key points and conclusions from the preceding discussion. In addition, the chapter will emphasise that although the criminal justice system plays an essential role in addressing domestic abuse, providing an effective response to this issue requires a holistic approach involving other aspects such as the provision of sufficient funding for specialist services.

Terminology

Although the term 'victims' of domestic abuse is used consistently throughout this book, the author recognises that there is a debate regarding whether the term 'survivor' is more appropriate. For example, Burton remarks that, '"Survivor" does perhaps have more positive connotations than "victim"; it is suggestive of the many ways that women cope with domestic violence and the strength they show in resisting it'.[14] Nevertheless, as Lewis states, 'many women do not feel like survivors at points in their lives, and…some do not survive men's violence'.[15]

Also, the terms 'domestic abuse' and 'domestic violence' tend to be used interchangeable in the relevant bodies of literature. The book uses the term 'domestic abuse' as this approach is consistent with the terminology used in the Domestic Abuse and Civil Proceedings Act (Northern Ireland) 2021; however, a number of the sources cited use the term 'domestic violence'.[16]

In addition, although it is recognised that 'domestic abuse' can refer to abuse taking place between a wide range of family members, the book uses the term primarily to refer to abuse between intimate partners. The book does not focus exclusively on female victims of domestic abuse, although a number of the sources cited refer to female victims.[17] In particular, the statements of the UN bodies which are discussed in Chapter 2 conceptualise domestic abuse simply as a form of violence against women – domestic abuse against men has not been considered by any of the UN bodies to any substantive extent. Domestic abuse against men is however an important issue and one which should not be forgotten.[18]

Notes

1 UN Women, 'COVID-19 and Ending Violence Against Women and Girls', www.unwomen.org/-/media/headquarters/attachments/sections/library/publications/2020/issue-brief-covid-19-and-ending-violence-against-women-and-girls-en.pdf?la=en&vs=5006

2 McWilliams M. and Ní Aoláin F., '"There is a war going on you know": Addressing the complexity of violence against women in conflicted and post conflict societies', (2013) 1 *Transitional Justice Review* 4 at 27.

3 According to statistics released by the Police Service of Northern Ireland (PSNI), there were 31,848 domestic abuse incidents in Northern Ireland during 2020, one of the highest rates since such records began in 2004/05. (Northern Ireland Statistics and Research Agency 'Domestic Abuse Incidents and Crimes Recorded by the Police in Northern Ireland: Update to 31 December 2020' (25 February 2021), www.psni.police.uk/globalassets/inside-the-psni/our-statistics/domestic-abuse-statistics/2020-21/q3/domestic-abuse-bulletin-dec-20.pdf

4 Article 2(1) states that, 'Everyone's right to life shall be protected by law'.

5 Article 3 states that, 'No one shall be subjected to torture or to inhuman or degrading treatment or punishment'.

6 Article 8(1) states that, 'Everyone has the right to respect for his private and family life, his home and his correspondence'.

7 The relevant part of Article 14 states that, 'The enjoyment of the rights and freedoms set forth in this Convention shall be secured without discrimination on any ground such as sex …'.

8 See for example, *Bevacqua and S. v Bulgaria* (application no. 71127/01, judgment of 12 June 2008); *Opuz v Turkey* (application no. 33401/02, judgment of 9 June 2009); *E.S. and Others v Slovakia* (application no. 8227/04, judgment of 15 September 2009); *A v Croatia* (application no. 55164/08, judgment of 14 October 2010); *Hajduova v Slovakia* (application no. 2660/03, judgment of 30 November 2010); *Kalucza v Hungary* (application no. 57693/10, judgment of 24 April 2012); *Valiuliene v Lithuania* (application no. 33234/07, judgment of 26 March 2013); *Eremia and Others v Republic of Moldova* (application no. 3564/11, judgment of 28 May 2013); *M.G. v Turkey* (application no. 646/10, judgment of 22 March 2016); *Balsan v Romania* (application no. 49645/09, judgment of 23 May 2017); *Talpis v Italy* (application no. 41237/14, judgment of 18 September 2017); and *Volodina v Russia* (application no. 41261/17, judgment of 9 July 2019).

9 Application no. 62903/15, judgment of 15 June 2021.

10 Criminal Justice Inspection Northern Ireland, 'Domestic Violence and Abuse', December 2010, www.cjini.org/getattachment/1b651b43-657b-471b-b320-101fca7c6930/Domestic-Violence-and-Abuse.aspx;

Criminal Justice Inspection Northern Ireland, 'Domestic Violence and Abuse – A Follow Up Review', October 2013, www.cjini.org/getattachment/34118bcc-00c5-4071-bf2f-5397e6b20332/report.aspx; Criminal Justice Inspection Northern Ireland, 'No Excuse', June 2019, www.cjini.org/getattachment/079beabb-d094-40e9-8738-0f84cd347ae8/report.aspx

11 Department of Justice, 'Domestic Abuse Offence and Domestic Violence Disclosure Scheme – A Consultation', 5 February 2016, www.justice-ni.gov.uk/sites/default/files/consultations/doj/consultation-domestic-violence.PDF

12 The Assembly is the devolved legislature for Northern Ireland which was established as a result of the Good Friday Agreement (or Belfast Agreement) of 10 April 1998, following talks between the Northern Ireland political parties and the British and Irish Governments. The Agreement was given legal force through the Northern Ireland Act 1998. See further www.niassembly.gov.uk/about-the-assembly/history-of-the-assembly/

13 Crown Prosecution Service, 'Stalking Analysis Reveals Domestic Abuse Link', 4 December 2020, www.cps.gov.uk/cps/news/stalking-analysis-reveals-domestic-abuse-link

14 Burton M., *Legal Responses to Domestic Violence*, 2008, Routledge-Cavendish, Abingdon, at 124.

15 Lewis R., 'Making justice work: Effective legal interventions for domestic violence', (2004) 44 *British Journal of Criminology* 204.

16 For further discussion of the debates surrounding the relevant terminology, see Aldridge J., '"Not an either/or situation": The minimization of violence

against women in United Kingdom "domestic abuse" policy', (2021) 27 *Violence Against Women* 1823.

17 For discussion of gender and domestic abuse, see for example, Dobash R.P. and Dobash R.E., 'Women's violence to men in intimate relationships: Working on a puzzle', (2004) 44 *British Journal of Criminology* 324; Kimmel M.S., '"Gender symmetry" in domestic violence: A substantive and methodological research review', (2002) 6 *Violence Against Women* 1332; and Johnson M.P., 'Conflict and control: Gender symmetry and asymmetry in domestic violence', (2006) 12 *Violence Against Women* 1003.

18 For discussion of domestic violence against men, see Martin L., 'Debates of Difference: Male Victims of Domestic Violence and Abuse', in S. Hilder and V. Bettinson (eds.), *Domestic Violence – Interdisciplinary Perspectives on Protection, Prevention and Intervention*, 2016, Palgrave Macmillan, London, 181–201.

2 What Constitutes an Effective Criminal Justice Response to Domestic Abuse?

This chapter examines the factors which are necessary in order to provide an effective criminal justice response to domestic abuse. The chapter begins by discussing the difficulties involved in fitting the issue of domestic abuse into the criminal justice system, and then proceeds to examine the academic literature on what is needed in relation to providing an effective legislative response. Literature focusing on the roles played by three key constituent parts of the criminal justice system – the police, the prosecution service and the courts – is then discussed with the aim of establishing what is necessary in order for these agencies to provide effective responses to victims of domestic abuse.[1]

The chapter will then provide some background information on the conceptualisation of domestic abuse as an issue for international human rights law, and will proceed to discuss human rights standards regarding the provision of an effective criminal justice response to domestic abuse.[2] At the UN level, the statements which have been made by entities such as the Special Rapporteur on violence against women, its causes and consequences, and the CEDAW Committee will be examined. As regards the Council of Europe, the Istanbul Convention contains provisions which set out standards regarding effective criminal justice responses to domestic abuse. Although the UK has not yet ratified this instrument, it has nevertheless signed the Convention, thereby demonstrating its intention to become a party at a later date. Also, it has been established that domestic abuse can constitute a breach of Articles 2, 3, 8 and 14 of the ECHR, and the ECtHR has developed a considerable body of jurisprudence on the question of how criminal justice systems should respond to this issue.

DOI: 10.4324/9781003261650-2

Domestic Abuse and the Criminal Justice System

There have been difficulties with fitting the issue of domestic abuse into the criminal justice system. As Freedman comments, 'the criminal justice system is best at dealing with relatively straightforward examples and easily categorised domestic violence, with recognisable story lines and sympathetic victims'.[3] Such paradigmatic examples are emphasised to the detriment of cases that do not so easily fit the mould.[4] Many victims of domestic abuse simply do not trust the criminal justice system. Others may wish to continue the relationship, while the involvement of the criminal law assumes that the relationship has come to an end. As James remarks:

> Coming into the open with domestic violence is an extremely difficult thing for a victim to do. There is an inherent belief common among victims that what they are suffering is not serious enough to trouble the police and the courts with. In fact, quite often, they are convinced that to do so will make a bad situation worse.[5]

Essentially, the criminal justice system may not take account of the many complexities at play in relation to the issue of domestic abuse.[6] Freedman comments that:

> The criminal justice system concentrates its resources on the most serious, urgent and unambiguous cases, then labels one or both parties as deviant, and administers simple and easy to understand remedies, thereby providing a safe social distance between 'normal' families and those afflicted with domestic violence.[7]

Merry highlights that the involvement of the criminal justice system can be a humiliating experience, even for the victims of domestic abuse.[8] In addition, the victim is not legally represented in a criminal prosecution and has no control over the process.[9]

Nevertheless, it remains indisputable that the criminal justice system has a crucial role to play as regards domestic abuse. As Mullender and Hague comment, the police 'frequently top the list of agencies contacted by domestic violence survivors for help',[10] and that 'most women favour a strong criminal justice stance'.[11] They also remark that, 'survivors think domestic violence should be responded to as a crime, but need support and protection in order for this to be a viable option'.[12]

The Need for Effective Criminal Legislation

In order to provide an effective criminal justice response to domestic abuse, the first element that is needed is effective legislation on which such a response can be based. Approaches to criminalisation of domestic abuse vary as to whether the conduct involved is prosecuted under general criminal law statutes relating to offences against the person more broadly, or under specific domestic abuse offences.[13] For example, in Northern Ireland, until the passing of the Domestic Abuse and Civil Proceedings Act (Northern Ireland) 2021 in March 2021, there was no specific offence of domestic abuse in this jurisdiction. Instead, incidents of domestic abuse had to be prosecuted under general criminal law statutes such as the Offences Against the Person Act 1861. This was relatively unproblematic as regards incidents of physical violence, as these could be prosecuted under the 1861 Act as, for example, common assault under section 42, aggravated assault under section 43, assault occasioning actual bodily harm under section 47, assault occasioning grievous bodily harm under section 18 or unlawful wounding under section 20. In *R v Ireland; R v Burstow*[14] it was held that a recognisable psychiatric illness could constitute 'bodily harm' for the purposes of sections 18, 20 and 47 of the Offences Against the Person Act. Nevertheless, states of mind which are not supported by medical evidence of psychiatric injury are not encompassed by the 1861 legislation.

However, it has now been recognised that domestic abuse encompasses not only physical violence but also 'coercive control' more broadly.[15] As Herring remarks,

> The concept of coercive control is an attempt to identify one of the wrongs at the heart of domestic abuse. It does so by showing that domestic abuse is a particular kind of relationship rather than being a particular kind of act.[16]

Fitz-gibbon, Walklate and McCulloch comment that, 'Coercive control illuminates domestic abuse as a pattern of behaviours, within which physical violence may exist alongside a range of other abusive behaviours'.[17] As Women's Aid states, 'Coercive control creates invisible chains and a sense of fear that pervades all elements of a victim's life. It works to limit their human rights by depriving them of their liberty and reducing their ability for action'.[18] The tactics of perpetrators of coercive control may include emotional abuse such as blaming the victim or undermining her self-esteem and self-worth; verbal abuse such as humiliation and degradation; systematic social isolation; economic abuse, for example controlling all finances; threats and intimidation; and physical abuse.[19] As Herring comments, 'Fear is often at the heart of coercive control and is its primary vehicle. Violence may or may not, be used as one tool'.[20]

Debate has arisen as to whether it is beneficial for a State to enact a bespoke offence of domestic abuse. As Burton states, 'The issue of whether the criminal law should seek to distinguish between different forms of violence according to the context is a thorny one'.[21] The main argument against the enactment of such an offence is that it may serve to give the impression that domestic abuse is a family matter, and should be distinguished from other types of violence as being less serious. Burton remarks that:

> Symbolically the marking out of domestic violence as a distinctive wrong is defensible, but the educative value of the criminal law may be overstated if it is assumed that the separation of the offence can effectively communicate a message that domestic violence is a serious form of misconduct which the state will not tolerate.[22]

However, Tadros argues that there should be a specific offence of domestic abuse in order to identify the distinctive type of wrong which is involved.[23] As Youngs asserts, 'A compelling principle in favour of a specific offence is that of fair labelling'.[24] Additionally, it may encourage victims to seek help 'if the law communicates that what they have suffered is criminal'.[25] As Tolmie comments:

> Interpersonal violence offences are constructed primarily in terms of incidents. As a result the criminal justice system fragments long-standing patterns of IPV into separate offences…Each incident is taken out of the pattern in which it occurs and proven and responded to in isolation. A corollary of this point is that the criminal offences are primarily constructed in terms of the use of physical violence. This means that IPV is also stripped of much of its overall architecture – those aspects of the pattern of abuse that are psychological and financial, for example, along with the motivations of the abuser and the cumulative effect on the victim. As a consequence, the totality and meaning of the perpetrator's behaviour, the continuing risk he poses and the weight of harm experienced by the victim are all potentially misunderstood and minimized at every stage of the criminal justice process – investigation, charging, trial and sentencing.[26]

Likewise, Bettinson and Bishop assert that, ‘the creation of an offence of controlling or coercive behaviour in an intimate or family relationship is necessary in order for the criminal law to better reflect the reality of the central harm of domestic violence’.[27] As Youngs remarks:

> Domestic violence is a wrong qualitatively different from any other. Once its unique character is established, analysis reveals that the current law, in relation to both physical and psychological abuse, does not address the totality of harm suffered by victims, the sustained nature of the wrong or the intent of the perpetrator.[28]

It seems therefore that the first step to ensuring an effective criminal justice response to domestic abuse involves putting in place a foundation of legislation specific to this issue on which the responses of actors within the criminal justice system can then be based.

The Need for Effective Police Responses

Police forces undoubtedly play an immensely important role in the protection of victims of domestic abuse. As Stanko comments, ‘in cases of acute violence, police intervention is crucial – a woman’s life depends on it’.[29] Armatta states that:

> Police occupy a pivotal position in any criminal law strategy to address domestic violence. In most places, police are the only institution with twenty-four-hour and comprehensive geographic accessibility. They also bring the coercive power of the state to bear on volatile and potentially lethal situations.[30]

Likewise, Hague and Malos comment that:

> the police role in combating domestic violence is…essential, and their handling of violence cases is of key significance to abused women…because of the traumatic and crucial point at which they are being asked to intervene on women’s behalf.[31]

However, unhelpful police attitudes have historically constituted a considerable problem as regards responding to domestic abuse, in that police officers have been reluctant to intervene in such situations. A number of studies carried out in the UK during the late 1970s and early 1980s demonstrate the prevalence of such attitudes. For instance, in the report of research carried out by the University of Bradford in 1979, it was stated that:

> Although a man's home is his castle, and very little short of murdering his wife will make people feel justified in violating its privacy, the position is quite different if he has broken the law in some other way; if he is suspected of burglary, grievous bodily harm to an acquaintance or harming his own child, we forget his rights to privacy. It seems reasonable enough that if someone is breaking the law, they lose some of their rights to privacy at home, and that search warrants, for instance, are available. It is therefore very striking that the police, who are the group most often authorised to bypass social rules about privacy, show such respect for them when it comes to violence to wives and cohabitees.[32]

Essentially domestic abuse was regarded as being unlike other types of criminal behaviour, and even as not being truly 'criminal' in character. The study found that the police were very reluctant to violate the privacy of a perpetrator by intervening to protect the victim.

A study carried out by the Research and Planning Unit of the Home Office in 1989 uncovered similar findings.[33] In the report of the study it was stated that 'the single most common police response is non-intervention, that is, officers state that there is nothing they can do and leave the incident to which they have been called'.[34] The report found that a common occurrence in the UK was for the victim to be told that the abuse she had suffered was a matter for the civil law, as opposed to the criminal law. This was in line with attitudes whereby domestic abuse was regarded as being not truly 'criminal' in character. Other responses highlighted by the Home Office study included attempts to defuse the situation and the removal of one of the parties, often the victim, from the scene for a certain length of time.[35] The view of domestic abuse as not being criminal in nature was, as the Home Office study found, premised on the idea that 'domestic violence is almost exclusively a "family matter" or a "private affair" in which State intervention has no business since it would constitute not solely an intrusion into a private relationship but also an erosion of individual liberties'.[36]

Writing in 1997, Armatta commented that, 'police throughout the world often fail to enforce criminal assault laws where violence occurs within an intimate relationship. Traditionally, police simply do not intervene, or intervene only to mediate on an informal basis'.[37] In 2001 Mullender and Hague stated that, 'In many localities, women continue to report little change in criminal justice responses'.[38] Victims still felt at risk during the post-separation phase.[39] There were also reports that the attitudes of police officers outside Domestic Violence Units often contrasted greatly with those officers who worked within these Units.[40] Mullender and Hague commented that, 'This has implications for increased efforts to re-educate the wider and longer-serving police service that times have changed'.[41]

Also in 2001, Hanmer and Griffiths identified the essential difficulty as being, 'The low status of domestic violence as police work',[42] concluding that, 'Policies and guidance on policing domestic violence remain to be fully implemented'.[43] They argued that:

> Good practice issues to be considered in developing new cost effective approaches to domestic violence are improved reporting and increased satisfaction with policing on the part of those experiencing domestic violence, improvements in police organisation, training and management, including information management, audits and statistical reporting, and effective partnership approaches.[44]

Again in 2001, Hague, Mullender, Aris and Dear commented that, 'The rather mixed outcome in response to police improvements overall…supports the premise that, despite transformations in service in some areas, there is still a patchy performance within police services in relation to domestic violence'.[45]

In 2003 Sullivan stated that the police could not be relied upon to arrest the perpetrator in a domestic abuse situation.[46] In 2004 Goodmark made the point that in the US, 'Police officers frequently told abusive spouses to take a walk around the block to cool down and attempted to mediate between abusers and their victims'.[47] Writing in 2005, Hester and Westmarland commented that 'up to 50 per cent of incidents reported to the police may remain unrecorded',[48] and that, 'The "patchiness" of appropriate police responses to domestic violence still needs to be addressed'.[49] Also in 2005, Hague and Malos found that the responses of individual officers varied, as did the responses of different police stations.[50] In 2006 Hughes remarked that, 'Police forces may be unresponsive to requests for assistance from women on the receiving end of domestic violence, or they may adopt a non-interventionist approach, considering that it is a "private" matter'.[51] Writing in 2007, Connelly and Cavanagh commented that:

> the attitudes of too many police officers…in respect of domestic abuse and the difficulties encountered in enforcing civil protection

> orders, are based upon stereotypes which have long been associated with domestic abuse and women who are subjected to that abuse.[52]

The responses of the police in Northern Ireland to the issue of domestic abuse, both historically and currently, are discussed in Chapters 3 and 4.

It is of course acknowledged that the question of precisely what constitutes an effective police response to domestic abuse may not be entirely clear-cut. For example, it is possible to criticise pro-arrest policies as actually endangering victims.[53] As Mullender and Hague point out, not all victims want to see their partner arrested.[54] This may be because they love him or depend on him, however, 'Very frequently… the hesitation springs from fear of reprisals and repercussions from the perpetrator…because women simply do not feel safe'.[55] Nevertheless, Hanmer and Griffiths remark that:

> Arrest is a factor in identifying future chronic offenders as well as a response to common law offences and criminal assault. Arrest is a means of identifying men who are more violent and is useful in assessing the risk of future calls for assistance. Understanding the full potential of arrest as a policing strategy and integrating this into police work are major issues.[56]

Essentially, 'A major unresolved issue for policing is how to combine "victim sensitive" approaches with proactive strategies'.[57] Nevertheless, 'Discretion is an integral part of policing. In best practice, responses are tailored to individual circumstances within broad frameworks of policy and good practice guidelines'.[58]

The Need for Effective Prosecutorial Responses

Prosecution services also constitute vital components in ensuring effective criminal justice responses to domestic abuse. However, the negative attitudes which prosecutors have historically taken towards cases of domestic abuse have also been well-documented. According to a UN document of 1993,

> The decision to prosecute cases of domestic violence rests, in most jurisdictions, with the prosecutors' office which represents the State. These offices have not prosecuted most cases of domestic violence referred to them. Nor have they treated these cases in the same manner as cases involving violence between strangers.[59]

Writing in 1985, Stanko remarked upon the very strong belief among prosecutors that victims who said that they wanted to pursue cases against their abusive partners would frequently drop the charges.[60] Also, cases relating to domestic abuse were very likely to be dropped as they did not constitute 'the sort of successful prosecution which brings additional kudos'.[61] In 1996 Cretney and Davis stated that, 'The difficulty about domestic assault cases lies in the frailty, as prosecutors perceive it, of the woman's commitment to the prosecution enterprise'.[62] Of the cases that were prosecuted, Cretney and Davis commented that the charges were often reduced from assault occasioning actual bodily harm to common assault.[63] They argued that the idea that the criminal courts were not the correct forum for domestic abuse cases still persisted,[64] and that domestic abuse cases were 'still viewed by police, prosecutors and sentencers through the lens of "the couple" or "the family"'.[65] Writing in 1999 in the context of the US, Thomas commented that:

> If a domestic violence victim manages to reach the stage in the criminal justice process where she either seeks or requires the assistance or authority of the prosecutor's office, she frequently encounters a lack of enthusiasm or even hostility parallel to that which she found with the police.[66]

In 2001 Edwards found that the Crown Prosecution Service (CPS) was particularly likely to engage in 'plea-bargaining' in cases of domestic abuse,[67] and that, 'There is some evidence…that the CPS has not lived up to its own promise to always explore all possibilities before abandoning a prosecution'.[68] Edwards commented that, 'The likelihood of prosecution remains poor',[69] and that all efforts should be made to improve the probability of prosecution of domestic abuse cases as, 'Prosecution can reduce domestic violence and is instrumental in intervening in the escalation and repetition of such incidents'.[70] Also in 2001, Miles stated that, 'The opportunity to admit written evidence in lieu is…seldom taken by the prosecution, though some victims may be absent through a desire for reconciliation rather than fear'.[71]

In 2003 Hester, Hanmer, Coulson, Morahan and Razak interviewed victims of domestic abuse who had experienced the criminal justice system in the UK and found that they 'were generally bewildered and shocked by the plea-bargaining and reduction in sentences that tended to take place in court'.[72] They also found that in cases in which the parties were back together, 'the victim-witness was deemed less reliable and cases were more likely to be discontinued'.[73] Writing in 2005, Hester and Westmarland commented that, 'A lack of consistency in criminal justice practice has been found both in relation to individual professionals and in relation to geographical areas'.[74] In 2010 Hall remarked that:

> The difficulties of prosecuting domestic violence are well known and principally revolve around low reporting rates and the fact that, even when victims do come forward to the authorities, the perception is that complainants in such cases have a tendency to retract their initial police statement at a late stage and become unwilling to give evidence in court.[75]

As with police responses to domestic abuse, it must be acknowledged that the question of precisely what constitutes an effective prosecutorial response to domestic abuse may be somewhat open to debate. For example, one much discussed issue is that of whether a prosecution should continue even where the victim decides that she does not wish this to happen. Hague and Malos comment that in certain cases where the victim is the only witness, compelling her to give evidence may place her in danger. Nevertheless, policies of dropping prosecutions whenever a police officer or prosecutor is of the view that the victim may not wish to proceed are not helpful.[76] In the report of a Home Office Research Study on domestic abuse it was commented that:

> On the one hand, prosecution can be seen as likely to aggravate conflict between the partners in a relationship, perhaps leading to an escalation in violence. On the other hand, it can be argued that no violence, whether between family members or strangers, should be tolerated and that it is the responsibility of the whole of the criminal justice system, not just the police, to ensure this. Moreover, it can also be argued that the very nature of domestic violence – its recurrent nature, increasing frequency of attacks and escalating severity of each assault – makes prosecution even more appropriate.[77]

The report also stated that it is unlikely that a general practice of arrests without subsequent prosecutions would be a strong deterrent.[78]

The Need for Effective Judicial Responses

Effective judicial responses constitute another vital part of ensuring an effective criminal justice response to the issue of domestic abuse. As Berry comments, 'Judges who are committed to giving domestic violence priority as a serious crime can have a tremendous effect on both criminal justice and public attitudes'.[79] For instance, if a judge hands down stiff sentences to perpetrators of domestic abuse, a clear statement is made that such behaviour will not be tolerated. Also, the opinions of judges tend to be accorded respect in their local communities.[80] Hester and Westmarland remark that 'attrition may be lower where…judges or magistrates have domestic violence training'.[81]

However, historically the failure of judges to react positively to cases of domestic abuse has been problematic. Writing in 1999, Thomas stated that, 'judges from every region demonstrate a dangerous unwillingness to understand the causes and consequences of domestic violence and to enforce the laws against it'.[82] Again the difficulty has arisen of violence in the home being viewed as being less serious than violence between strangers. Also writing in 1999, Diduck and Kaganas commented that in the UK charges in domestic abuse cases were often reduced and bind-overs were commonly used. Reduced sentences tended to be handed down if the perpetrator was not viewed as a danger to the public. Factors such as the victim's infidelity may also have been taken into account. If the couple had not separated, the perpetrator was less likely to be convicted.[83]

Writing in 2001, Miles stated that conditional bail and remand were not always used efficiently by police and courts in order to protect victims from intimidation before trial.[84] Also in 2001, Edwards remarked that, 'when defendants are proceeded against and convicted at the sentencing stage magistrates and judges continue to pass derisory sentences'.[85] Again in 2001, Mullender, Hague, Aris and Dear found that the courts were one of the organisations least likely to respond appropriately to domestic abuse.[86] In 2003 Hester, Hanmer, Coulson, Morahan and Razak found that victims 'felt particularly let down by the court process and the frequently inadequate outcomes'.[87] Those interviewed said that, 'The fines and bind-overs, or short custodial sentences, did not stop the men continuing their violence and harassment in the longer term'.[88]

Domestic Abuse as an International Human Rights Issue

Prior to examining the standards laid down by international and regional human rights bodies as regards effective criminal justice responses to domestic abuse, it must first be noted that it is only relatively recently that domestic abuse began to be regarded as an issue for human rights law. The primary difficulty in this regard lay in the manner in which the rights themselves were formulated. As Fredman comments, 'Human rights have long been understood as providing protection for individual freedom against an intrusive State'.[89] Rights therefore developed in such a way as to create a public/private divide by which human rights norms were upheld in the public sphere where the State was involved, but were not applied in the private sphere. As Burton remarks, 'In the classic public/private dichotomy intimate relationships are seen as part of the "private" sphere not suitable for public regulation'.[90]

Nevertheless, the public/private dichotomy does not now pose an insurmountable difficulty for the recognition of domestic abuse as an issue for human rights law. The concept of State responsibility has been developed, under which positive obligations can be placed on the State to ensure that human rights standards are upheld in situations involving only private individuals. For instance, the UN human rights bodies often refer to the State's duties to respect, protect, promote and fulfil rights. Although none of the UN human rights treaties make any express reference to domestic abuse, in 1992 the CEDAW Committee issued General Recommendation No. 19 which interpreted the UN Convention on the Elimination of All Forms of Discrimination Against Women (CEDAW) as prohibiting violence against women in both the public and private spheres. General Recommendation No. 19 stated that, 'The full implementation of the Convention required States to take positive measures to eliminate all forms of violence against women'.[91] The General Recommendation proceeded to assert that:

> The definition of discrimination includes gender-based violence, that is, violence that is directed against a woman because she is a woman or that affects women disproportionately. It includes acts that inflict physical, mental or sexual harm or suffering, threats of such acts, coercion and other deprivations of liberty. Gender-based violence may breach specific provisions of the Convention, regardless of whether those provisions expressly mention violence.[92]

The General Recommendation stated that gender-based violence may breach *inter alia* the right to life; the right not to be subject to torture or to cruel, inhuman or degrading treatment or punishment; and the right to liberty and security of person.[93] It emphasised that:

> discrimination under the Convention is not restricted to action by or on behalf of Governments...Under general international law and specific human rights covenants, States may be responsible for private acts if they fail to act with due diligence to prevent violations of rights or to investigate and punish acts of violence, and for providing compensation.[94]

The General Recommendation also asserted that:

> Family violence is one of the most insidious forms of violence against women. It is prevalent in all societies. Within family relationships women of all ages are subjected to violence of all kinds, including battering, rape, other forms of sexual assault, mental and other forms of violence, which are perpetuated by traditional attitudes.[95]

In 1993, the UN General Assembly issued the UN Declaration on the Elimination of Violence against Women,[96] which emphasised the need to address the issue of domestic abuse in order to protect the right to life; the right not to be subjected to torture, or other cruel, inhuman or degrading treatment or punishment; the right to equality; the right to liberty and security of person; the right to equal protection under the law; the right to be free from all forms of discrimination; and the right to the highest standard attainable of physical and mental health.[97]

Following the World Conference on Human Rights which was held in Vienna in 1993,[98] a Special Rapporteur on violence against women, its causes and consequences, was appointed by the UN Commission on Human Rights. It has been commented that the Special Rapporteur 'brought international consciousness to a new level'.[99] The first holder of the post, Radhika Coomaraswamy, was appointed in 1994, and in 1996 she produced a framework for model legislation on domestic violence.[100]

The Fourth World Conference on Women was held in 1995 in Beijing, with the resulting Platform for Action urging States to adopt a wide range of measures regarding violence against women.[101] In addition, the UN Commission on Human Rights and the Human Rights Council which succeeded it, have also issued statements relevant to domestic abuse.[102]

Overall, various categories of recommendations have been made to States by the UN bodies in terms of responding to domestic abuse. These include the adoption of measures relating to improving their criminal justice systems; improving measures of civil protection; providing social support measures for victims; increasing awareness within society regarding issues surrounding domestic abuse; increasing awareness of professionals who may be particularly likely to come into contact with victims; and developing programmes for perpetrators.[103] In addition, the CEDAW Committee has now considered a number of complaints in relation to the responses of States to domestic abuse which have been taken under the Optional Protocol procedure,[104] which enables individuals or groups to submit to the Committee claims of breaches of CEDAW.

The growing recognition of domestic abuse as being an issue for human rights law is not of course confined to the UN system. In 1994 the Inter-American Convention on the Prevention, Punishment and Eradication of Violence against Women (Convention of Belém do Pará) was adopted by the General Assembly of the Organization of American States (OAS). In addition, the Protocol to the African Charter on Human and Peoples' Rights on the Rights of Women in Africa (Maputo Protocol), which encompasses *inter alia* violence against women, was adopted by the African Union in 2003. As regards the Council of Europe, the European Court of Human Rights has directly addressed the issue of domestic abuse in a series of cases,[105] and it has been established that domestic abuse can violate the right to life, as found in Article 2 of the ECHR; the right to be free from torture and inhuman or degrading treatment, as found in Article 3; the right to respect for one's private and family life, as found in Article 8; and the Article 14 equality provision.[106] In addition, in 2011 the Council of Europe adopted the Convention on Preventing and Combating Violence Against Women and Domestic Violence (Istanbul Convention).[107]

Human Rights Standards on Effective Criminal Justice Responses to Domestic Abuse

At the UN level, attention has been paid to the need to provide effective criminal justice responses to domestic abuse for quite some time. For example, as far back as 1980, the Report of the World Conference of the United Nations Decade for Women: Equality, Development and Peace, which was held in Copenhagen, stated that, 'Legislation should...be enacted and implemented in order to prevent domestic and sexual violence against women. All appropriate measures, including legislative ones, should be taken to allow victims to be fairly treated in all criminal procedures'.[108] In 1985, the UN General Assembly issued a Resolution on domestic abuse in which it invited States to 'adopt specific measures with a view to making the criminal and civil justice system more sensitive in its response to domestic violence, and to enact and enforce such laws in order to protect battered family members and punish the offender'; and also to 'respect, in all instances of the criminal proceeding, starting with the police investigation, the special and sometimes delicate position of the victim, in particular in the manner in which the victim is treated'.[109]

Also, the Report of the World Conference to Review and Appraise the Achievements of the United Nations Decade for Women: Equality, Development and Peace, which was held in Nairobi in 1985, stated that:

> Special attention should be given in criminology training to the particular situation of women as victims of violent crimes, including crimes that violate women's bodies and result in serious physical and psychological damage. Legislation should be passed and laws enforced in every country to end the degradation of women through sex-related crimes. Guidance should be given to law enforcement and other authorities on the need to deal sensibly and sensitively with the victims of such crimes.[110]

In 1990, the UN General Assembly issued another Resolution on domestic abuse in which it recommended that States 'ensure that their systems of criminal justice...provide an effective and equitable response to domestic violence and that they take appropriate steps towards this goal'.[111]

As noted above, General Recommendation No. 19, which was issued by the CEDAW Committee in 1992, was an extremely important document in that it interpreted CEDAW in such a manner as to prohibit violence against women, both in the public context and in the private sphere. Nevertheless, in relation to the measures that States should take to improve the responses of their criminal justice systems to cases of domestic abuse, the General Recommendation was somewhat brief. It stated that measures necessary to overcome family violence included 'criminal penalties where necessary'[112] and that 'states parties should ensure that laws against family violence and abuse...give adequate protection to all women, and respect their integrity and dignity'.[113] There was no indication however as to how States should ensure that laws against domestic abuse should respect the 'integrity and dignity' of all women. It is nevertheless notable that the General Recommendation recognised that 'coercion' can amount to gender-based violence.[114]

The UN Declaration on the Elimination of Violence against Women, which was issued by the General Assembly in 1993, asserted that States should,

> Develop penal, civil, labour and administrative sanctions in domestic legislation to punish and redress the wrongs caused to women who are subjected to violence; women who are subjected to violence should be provided with access to the mechanisms of

> justice and, as provided for by national legislation, to just and effective remedies for the harm that they have suffered; States should also inform women of their rights in seeking redress through such mechanisms.[115]

The Declaration also asserted that States should,

> Develop, in a comprehensive way, preventive approaches and all those measures of a legal...nature that promote the protection of women against any form of violence, and ensure that the re-victimization of women does not occur because of laws insensitive to gender considerations, enforcement practices or other interventions.[116]

The Platform for Action which resulted from the Fourth World Conference on Women which was held in 1995 in Beijing, contained significant consideration of how the criminal justice systems of States should respond to domestic abuse. According to the Platform for Action, States should, 'exercise due diligence to prevent, investigate and, in accordance with national legislation, punish acts of violence against women, whether those acts are perpetrated by the State or by private persons';[117] and 'Enact and/or reinforce penal...sanctions in domestic legislation to punish and redress the wrongs done to women and girls who are subjected to any form of violence, whether in the home, the workplace, the community or society'.[118] States should also,

> Adopt and/or implement and periodically review and analyse legislation to ensure its effectiveness in eliminating violence against women, emphasizing the prevention of violence and the prosecution of offenders; take measures to ensure the protection of women subjected to violence, access to just and effective remedies, including compensation and indemnification and healing of victims, and rehabilitation of perpetrators.[119]

In addition, States should implement measures aimed at increasing the knowledge and understanding of law enforcement officers, police personnel and the judiciary in relation to the causes, consequences and mechanisms of violence against women among law enforcement officers, police personnel and the judiciary; and should 'develop strategies to ensure that the revictimization of women victims of violence does not occur because of gender-insensitive laws or judicial or enforcement practices'.[120] States should also, 'Provide women who are subjected to violence with access to the mechanisms of justice and, as provided for by national legislation, to just and effective remedies for the harm they have suffered and inform women of their rights in seeking redress through such mechanisms';[121] and 'Create or strengthen institutional mechanisms so that women and girls can report acts of violence against them in a safe and confidential environment, free from the fear of penalties or retaliation, and file charges'.[122]

The framework for model legislation on domestic violence which was produced by the UN Special Rapporteur on violence against women in 1996 dealt in a relatively detailed manner with how a State's criminal justice system should respond to cases of domestic abuse. For example, in relation to complaint mechanisms it was stated that:

> The law shall provide for victims, witnesses of domestic violence, family members and close associates of victims, State and private medical service providers and domestic violence assistance centres to complain of incidents of domestic violence to the police or file action in court.[123]

The duties of police officers in domestic abuse cases were laid down in detail. For example, the law should provide that police officers should respond to every request for assistance in cases of alleged domestic abuse.[124] Also, police officers should not regard calls concerning alleged domestic abuse as being of a lower priority than calls alleging violence by strangers.[125] The police should respond promptly even where the person reporting the incident was not the victim, but was a witness of the abuse, a friend of the victim or a professional working at a domestic abuse assistance centre.[126] Police officers should interview the parties in separate rooms,[127] record the details of the complaint,[128] advise the victim of her rights[129] and arrange transport for the victim to a medical facility if necessary.[130] The police should also arrange transport for the victim and her children to a shelter, if this is required.[131] The offender should be removed from the home or, if this is not possible and the victim remains in danger, the offender should be arrested.[132]

In addition, the police officer must provide the victim with a written statement outlining all the legal procedures available to her.[133] Essentially the police must take all reasonable measures to ensure that the victim is safe.[134] The Special Rapporteur also laid down the particulars that should be included in a report of an incident involving domestic abuse.[135] The police commissioner should compile annually the data collected from the domestic abuse reports and submit a summary report to Parliament.[136]

Furthermore, the Special Rapporteur laid down proper practice for prosecutors and courts in cases involving domestic abuse. For example, if a court dismisses criminal charges, the specific reasons for dismissal should be recorded.[137] During the course of the trial, the defendant should have no unsupervised contact with the plaintiff.[138] Clear sentencing guidelines should be established[139] and an order for counselling should not be made in place of a sentence in cases involving aggravated assault.[140]

In 2001 the UN Commission on Human Rights issued a Resolution on the elimination of violence against women in which the Commission called upon States,

> To enact and, where necessary, reinforce or amend penal…sanctions in domestic legislation to punish and redress the wrongs done to women and girls subjected to any form of violence, whether in the home, the workplace, the community or society…to ensure that they conform with relevant international human rights instruments… and to take action to investigate and punish persons who perpetrate acts of violence against women.[141]

In 2004 the Commission on Human Rights issued another Resolution on the elimination of violence against women in which it stressed that States 'have an affirmative duty to promote and protect the human rights and fundamental freedoms of women and girls and must exercise due diligence to prevent, investigate and punish all acts of violence against women and girls'.[142] The Commission proceeded to call upon States,

> To intensify efforts to develop and/or utilize legislative…and other measures aimed at the prevention of violence against women and to ensure women's full and equal access to justice, including the adoption and implementation of laws…and training of legal, judicial and health personnel on gender-based violence and related issues.[143]

States should also,

> enact and, where necessary, reinforce or amend domestic legislation, including measures to enhance the protection of victims, to investigate, prosecute, punish and redress the wrongs done to women and girls subjected to any form of violence, whether in the

> home, the workplace, the community or society...to ensure that such legislation conforms with relevant international human rights instruments...and to take action to investigate and punish persons who perpetrate acts of violence against women.[144]

In 2003 the UN General Assembly adopted a Resolution on 'Elimination of domestic violence against women' in which it stressed that:

> States have an obligation to exercise due diligence to prevent, investigate and punish the perpetrators of domestic violence against women and to provide protection to the victims, and...that not to do so violates and impairs or nullifies the enjoyment of their human rights and fundamental freedoms.[145]

The Resolution also reaffirmed the commitment of States 'to establish legislation and/or strengthen appropriate mechanisms to handle criminal matters relating to all forms of domestic violence, including marital rape and sexual abuse of women and girls, and to ensure that such cases are brought to justice swiftly'.[146] The General Assembly then proceeded to call upon States to,

> adopt, strengthen and implement legislation that prohibits domestic violence, prescribes punitive measures and establishes adequate legal protection against domestic violence and periodically to review, evaluate and revise these laws and regulations so as to ensure their effectiveness in eliminating domestic violence.[147]

States should also 'adopt and/or strengthen policies and legislation in order to strengthen preventive measures, protect the human rights of victims, ensure proper investigation and prosecution of perpetrators and provide legal and social assistance to victims of domestic violence';[148] 'provide or facilitate the provision of adequate training, inter alia, gender-awareness training, to all professionals who deal with domestic violence, ...police officers, judicial and legal personnel';[149] 'provide or facilitate the provision of assistance to victims of domestic violence in lodging police reports';[150] 'protect women in the process of seeking redress from further victimization because of gender-insensitive laws or practices';[151] and 'establish and/or strengthen police response protocols and procedures to ensure that all appropriate actions are taken to protect victims of domestic violence and to prevent further acts of domestic violence'.[152]

In 2006 the General Assembly adopted a Resolution on 'Intensification of efforts to eliminate all forms of violence against women' in which it stressed that:

> States have the obligation to promote and protect all human rights and fundamental freedoms of women and girls and must exercise due diligence to prevent, investigate and punish the perpetrators of violence against women and girls and to provide protection to the victims, and that failure to do so violates and impairs or nullifies the enjoyment of their human rights and fundamental freedoms.[153]

The General Assembly proceeded to urge States to

> end impunity for violence against women, by prosecuting and punishing all perpetrators, by ensuring that women have equal protection of the law and equal access to justice and by holding up to public scrutiny and eliminating those attitudes that foster, justify or tolerate violence.[154]

In 2017 the CEDAW Committee issued its General Recommendation No. 35 on gender-based violence against women,[155] which is essentially an updated and considerably more detailed version of the Committee's very influential General Recommendation No. 19.[156] General Recommendation No. 35 asserts that:

> States are required to adopt legislation prohibiting all forms of gender-based violence against women and girls, harmonising domestic law with the Convention. This legislation should consider women victims/survivors as right holders and include age and gender-sensitive provisions and effective legal protection, including sanctions and reparation in cases of such violence.[157]

States must also,

> Ensure that all forms of gender-based violence against women in all spheres, which amount to a violation of their physical, sexual, or psychological integrity, are criminalized and introduce, without delay, or strengthen legal sanctions commensurate with the gravity of the offence as well as civil remedies.[158]

All legal systems must protect victims and ensure that they have access to justice and to an effective remedy.[159] States should,

> Ensure effective access of victims to courts and tribunals; ensure authorities adequately respond to all cases of gender-based violence against women, including by applying criminal law and as appropriate ex officio prosecution to bring the alleged perpetrators to trial in a fair, impartial, timely and expeditious manner and imposing adequate penalties.[160]

According to the General Recommendation,

> all judicial bodies are required to refrain from engaging in any act or practice of discrimination or gender-based violence against women; and to strictly apply all criminal law provisions punishing this violence, ensuring all legal procedures in cases involving allegations of gender-based violence against women are impartial and fair, and unaffected by gender stereotypes or discriminatory interpretation of legal provisions.[161]

States should, 'Adopt and implement effective measures to protect and assist women complainants and witnesses of gender-based violence before, during and after legal proceedings' including through protecting their privacy and safety and implementing gender-sensitive court procedures and measures.[162] States should also ensure access to free or low-cost legal aid of a high quality,[163] and all legal proceedings should respect and strengthen the autonomy of victims.[164]

It can be seen therefore that at the UN level, recommendations have clearly been made to States to improve the responses of their criminal justice systems to cases involving domestic abuse. Such recommendations have also been made to States at the regional level. For example, the Istanbul Convention contains detailed consideration of how the criminal justice systems of States Parties should respond to the issue of domestic abuse. It is notable that the Convention does not require that States enact a specific offence of 'domestic abuse', however States Parties have a duty to ensure that conduct which constitutes domestic abuse is criminalised. Under Articles 35 and 36 of the Convention, physical and sexual violence must be criminalised through legislative or other measures. Article 33 states that, 'Parties shall take the necessary legislative or other measures to ensure that the intentional conduct of seriously impairing a person's psychological integrity through coercion or threats is criminalised'. Under Article 78(3), when signing or ratifying the Convention, a State Party may declare that it reserves the right to provide for non-criminal sanctions, instead of criminal sanctions, for the behaviours referred to in Article 33. At the time of writing however, only one of the current States Parties to the Convention has entered such a reservation.[165]

Article 46 of the Istanbul Convention sets out a list of factors which should be taken into consideration as aggravating circumstances in the determination of the sentence in relation to the offences established in accordance with the Convention. These include a number of factors which may have particular relevance to offences relating to domestic abuse, for example, if the offence was committed against a former or current spouse or partner, by a member of the family, a person cohabiting with the victim or a person having abused her or his authority;[166] if the offence, or related offences, were committed repeatedly;[167] if the offence was committed against a person made vulnerable by particular circumstances;[168] if the offence was committed against or in the presence of a child;[169] if the offence was preceded or accompanied by extreme levels of violence;[170] if the offence was committed with the use or threat of a weapon;[171] if the offence resulted in severe physical or psychological harm for the victim;[172] and if the perpetrator had previously been convicted of offences of a similar nature.[173]

Article 49(1) of the Convention states that:

> Parties shall take the necessary legislative or other measures to ensure that investigations and judicial proceedings in relation to all forms of violence covered by the scope of this Convention are carried out without undue delay while taking into consideration the rights of the victim during all stages of the criminal proceedings.

Under Article 49(2), States Parties must adopt 'the necessary legislative or other measures, in conformity with the fundamental principles of human rights and having regard to the gendered understanding of violence, to ensure the effective investigation and prosecution of offences established in accordance with this Convention'. According to the Explanatory Report to the Convention, 'This means, for example, establishing the relevant facts, interviewing all available witnesses, and conducting forensic examinations, based on a multi-disciplinary approach and using state-of-the-art criminal investigative methodology to ensure a comprehensive analysis of the case'.[174] Under Article 50, States Parties must ensure that law enforcement agencies respond promptly and appropriately to instances of violence against women by offering adequate and immediate protection to victims. Article 51 provides that in such cases, assessments must be carried out as regards the seriousness of the situation and the risk of repeated violence. As stated in the Explanatory Report, 'Concerns for the victim's safety must lie at the heart of any intervention in cases of all forms of violence covered by the scope of this Convention'.[175] Under Article 52,

> Parties shall take the necessary legislative or other measures to ensure that the competent authorities are granted the power to order, in situations of immediate danger, a perpetrator of domestic violence to vacate the residence of the victim or person at risk for a sufficient period of time and to prohibit the perpetrator from entering the residence of or contacting the victim or person at risk.

Under Article 55(1), States Parties must ensure that prosecutions of offences involving violence against women are not wholly dependent upon complaints being filed by victims, and that the proceedings may continue even if the victim withdraws her complaint. Again this is an issue of particular relevance to domestic abuse. In many cases, victims do not wish to have their assailants prosecuted due to a variety of reasons, such as a belief that a prosecution will simply lead to an escalation of violence. As noted previously, the question of whether a prosecution should proceed even without the consent of the victim is an extremely difficult issue. Should the wishes of the victim be respected in all cases or are there some instances in which the abuse is simply so horrific that intervention is essential regardless of the victim's views? In such cases, is a prosecution necessary in the interests of society? The Convention does not attempt to lay down guidelines as regards the circumstances in which prosecutions should proceed without the victim's consent – it simply states that it must be possible for this to happen. Nevertheless, it has to be remembered that the question of how to balance punishing offenders with protecting victims in cases of domestic abuse is very controversial. There does not appear to be any real consensus among those working in the field of domestic abuse as to how to proceed in a case in which a victim of severe domestic abuse does not wish her assailant to be prosecuted. It is perhaps too much to expect a human rights treaty to arrive at a definitive conclusion on this issue, as it is certainly arguable that it is not the function of human rights bodies to make decisions regarding such controversial details of policy.[176]

Nevertheless, the obligations placed on States Parties as regards the responses of their criminal justice systems to instances of violence against women are described in an impressive amount of detail. Article 55(2) states that:

> Parties shall take the necessary legislative or other measures to ensure, in accordance with the conditions provided for by their

> internal law, the possibility for governmental and non-governmental organisations and domestic violence counsellors to assist and/or support victims, at their request, during investigations and judicial proceedings concerning the offences established in accordance with this Convention.

As noted in the Explanatory Report,

> Good practice examples have shown that victims who are supported or assisted by a specialist support service during investigations and proceedings are more likely to file a complaint and testify and are better equipped to take on the emotionally challenging task of actively contributing to the outcome of proceedings.[177]

Under Article 56(1), victims must be informed, at least in cases where they may be in danger, if the perpetrator escapes from detention or is released.[178] Victims must also be informed of their rights and the services at their disposal, and of the progress of the investigation or proceedings.[179] They must be enabled to supply evidence and have their views and concerns presented and considered.[180] Contact between victims and perpetrators within court and law enforcement agency premises should be avoided where possible.[181] Measures should also be adopted to enable victims to testify in court without being present or without the presence of the alleged perpetrator, through the use of appropriate communication technologies, where available.[182]

The need for adequate criminal law measures to be adopted is also recognised in the Convention of Belém do Pará, of which Article 8(b) places a duty on States Parties to 'apply due diligence to prevent, investigate and impose penalties for violence against women'. Under Article 8(c), States Parties must 'include in their domestic legislation penal... provisions...to prevent, punish and eradicate violence against women'. Likewise, under Article 4(2) of the Maputo Protocol, States Parties must take appropriate and effective measures to 'enact and enforce laws to prohibit all forms of violence against women...whether the violence takes place in private or public';[183] 'adopt such other legislative... measures as may be necessary to ensure the prevention, punishment and eradication of all forms of violence against women';[184] and 'punish the perpetrators of violence against women'.[185]

In addition, the European Court of Human Rights has built up a substantial body of jurisprudence on domestic abuse. Since 2007, the Court has regularly issued judgments addressing this issue, and violations of Articles 2,[186] 3,[187] 8[188] and 14[189] of the ECHR have been found in such cases. It is noteworthy that in the case of *Volodina v Russia*,[190] the ECtHR recognised that the feelings of anxiety, fear and powerlessness which are caused by coercive and controlling behaviour can amount to inhuman treatment under Article 3. All of the breaches of the ECHR which have been established in the Court's jurisprudence on the issue of domestic abuse relate to failings on the part of the criminal justice systems of the States in question.

Particular attention has been paid to police responses, and to the application of the so-called '*Osman* test' to instances of domestic abuse. This was in fact a key aspect of the Grand Chamber's judgment in the recent case of *Kurt v Austria*,[191] which was the first case involving domestic abuse to be considered by the Grand Chamber of the ECtHR.

The '*Osman* test' was derived from the judgment of the ECtHR which was issued in 1998 in the case of *Osman v United Kingdom*.[192] The facts of this case involved a teacher who had wounded a student to whom he had developed an inappropriate attachment, and who had also killed the student's father. Prior to this incident he had carried out attacks on the family's property and threatened the deputy head teacher who had expressed serious concerns regarding his behaviour. The question to be considered by the ECtHR was whether the State should be held liable for breaching Article 2, the right to life, due to failings on the part of the police to respond in an adequate manner. In its judgment, the ECtHR stated that Article 2 requires the State 'not only to refrain from the "intentional" taking of life, but also to take appropriate steps to safeguard the lives of those within its jurisdiction'.[193] This positive obligation encompasses a duty on the State to put in place a legislative and administrative framework designed to provide effective deterrence against threats to the right of life. Also, in appropriate circumstances there is a positive obligation on the authorities to take preventive operational measures to protect an individual whose life is at risk from the criminal acts of another individual. The Court proceeded to assert that:

> bearing in mind the difficulties involved in policing modern societies, the unpredictability of human conduct and the operational choices which must be made in terms of priorities and resources, the obligation to take preventive operational measures to protect an individual whose life is at risk from the criminal acts of another individual must be interpreted in a way which does not impose an impossible or disproportionate burden on the authorities. Accordingly, not every claimed risk to life can entail for the

> authorities a Convention requirement to take operational measures to prevent that risk from materialising.[194]

Indeed, for such a positive obligation to arise,

> it must be established that the authorities knew or ought to have known at the time of the existence of a real and immediate risk to the life of an identified individual from the criminal acts of a third party and that they failed to take measures within the scope of their powers which, judged reasonably, might have been expected to avoid that risk.[195]

Since the decision of the ECtHR in *Osman*, the need for knowledge on the part of the authorities of such a 'real and immediate risk' to life in order to engage their duty to take reasonable measures to avoid such a risk, has been referred to by the Court in all cases in which the actions of State authorities such as the police have been scrutinised in instances relating to the deaths of individuals due to the criminal acts of third parties, including in circumstances involving domestic abuse.

However, there has been some debate regarding whether the *Osman* test is appropriate in cases of domestic abuse. For example, in the Chamber judgment in *Kurt v Austria*, one of the judges, Judge Huseynov, issued a concurring opinion in which he stated that, 'the relevance of this test is questionable in the particular context of domestic violence, that is to say, in cases where domestic violence has fatal results'.[196] Judge Huseynov proceeded to comment that:

> It is widely recognised that domestic violence often constitutes not just an isolated incident, but rather a continuous practice of intimidation and abuse. Therefore the State authorities should react, with due diligence, to each and every act of domestic violence and take all necessary measures to make sure that such acts do not lead to more serious consequences. It follows that the duty to prevent and protect comes into play when the risk to life is present, even if it is not imminent. In other words, in a domestic violence case, the positive obligation to protect life can be violated even where the risk to life is not immediate.[197]

Essentially, domestic abuse rarely consists of a single incident, but usually comprises an ongoing cycle. Therefore, even if the risk to life in such a case does not seem to be immediate, there is a substantial possibility that this could escalate at any point.

Likewise, in *Valiuliene v Lithuania*,[198] a 2013 case involving domestic abuse, Judge Pinto De Albuquerque gave a concurring judgment in which he commented in relation to the *Osman* test that:

> Realistically speaking, at the stage of an 'immediate risk' to the victim it is often too late for the State to intervene. In addition, the recurrence and escalation inherent in most cases of domestic violence makes it somehow artificial, even deleterious, to require an immediacy of the risk. Even though the risk might not be imminent, it is already a serious risk when it is present.[199]

In *Volodina v Russia*,[200] Judge Pinto De Albuquerque gave a separate opinion in which he further elaborated on this point, stating that:

> A 'real and immediate risk' in the context of domestic violence infers that the risk, namely the batterer, is already in the direct vicinity of the victim and about to strike the first blow. Were the test to be applied in such a manner, two concerns arise. Firstly, any protective action offered by the State would be too late and secondly, the State would have a legitimate excuse for not acting in a timely manner, since it is implausible to assume that the victim will be constantly accompanied by a State agent who may jump in to help. Hence, the 'immediacy' of the *Osman* test does not serve well in the context of domestic violence.[201]

In *Kurt v Austria*, the Grand Chamber took the opportunity to set out in some detail the positive obligations of the State under Article 2 in the context of domestic abuse, and focused in particular on how the *Osman* test should be applied in such cases. In this regard, the Grand Chamber stated that, 'The existence of a real and immediate risk to life…must be assessed taking due account of the particular context of domestic violence', and proceeded to clarify 'what it means to take into account the specific context and dynamics of domestic violence under the *Osman* test'.[202] Firstly, the Grand Chamber stated that 'an immediate response to allegations of domestic violence is required from the authorities',[203] and that 'special diligence is required from the authorities when dealing with cases of domestic violence'.[204] The judgment then noted that

> in order to be in a position to know whether there is a real and immediate risk to the life of a victim of domestic violence…the

> authorities are under a duty to carry out a lethality risk assessment which is autonomous, proactive and comprehensive.[205]

In doing so, the authorities should 'not rely solely on the victim's perception of the risk, but...complement it by their own assessment'.[206] The Grand Chamber emphasised the importance of regular training for authorities dealing with victims, in terms of understanding the dynamics of domestic abuse, thus enabling them to better assess any risk and to respond in an appropriate manner. Also, 'where several persons are affected by domestic violence, be it directly or indirectly, any risk assessment must be apt to systematically identify and address all the potential victims'.[207]

As regards the interpretation of the term 'immediate' in the *Osman* test, the Grand Chamber stated that 'the application of the immediacy standard in this context should take into account the specific features of domestic violence cases, and the ways in which they differ from incident-based situations' such as that which pertained in the *Osman* case itself.[208] In particular, 'consecutive cycles of domestic violence, often with an increase in frequency, intensity and danger over time, are frequently observed patterns in that context'.[209]

If it is established that there is a real and immediate risk to the life of one or more identified individuals, the positive obligation on the part of the State authorities to take operational measures is then triggered. In this respect, the Grand Chamber asserted that, 'the toolbox of legal and operational measures available must give the authorities involved a range of sufficient measures to choose from, which are adequate and proportionate to the level of (lethal) risk that has been assessed'.[210]

As will be discussed in Chapter 4, since March 2020 there has been a considerable rise in the levels of domestic abuse at the global level, in the context of the COVID-19 pandemic and the resulting lockdown measures which have been imposed by States.[211] In the context of this crisis, many victims of domestic abuse have found themselves to be even more isolated in such situations; and the anxieties caused by the pandemic in terms of health concerns and financial worries have increased tensions within many relationships, all too often resulting in violence. Various statements have been issued by UN and regional human rights bodies in response to these increased levels of domestic abuse. For example, in March 2020, the UN Special Rapporteur on violence against women, its causes and consequences issued a statement on domestic abuse in the context of COVID-19 lockdowns.[212] In this statement she called upon governments not to put the protection of victims on hold and urged them to continue to combat domestic abuse in the time of COVID-19. The Special Rapporteur asserted that, 'Governments must not allow the extraordinary circumstances and restrictive measures against COVID-19 to lead to the violation of women's right to a life free from violence'. In April 2020, the CEDAW Committee issued a guidance note on CEDAW and COVID-19, in which it emphasised that even during the circumstances of the pandemic, States Parties still had 'a due diligence obligation to prevent and protect women from, and hold perpetrators accountable for, gender-based violence against women'.[213] States should therefore ensure that victims of gender-based violence still had effective access to justice.[214] Under Article 66(1) of the Istanbul Convention, implementation of this instrument is monitored by the Group of Experts on Action against Violence against Women and Domestic Violence, known as 'GREVIO'. In March 2020, the President of GREVIO stated that the provisions of the Istanbul Convention continued to apply to all States Parties, 'be it in times of conflict or in times of a pandemic',[215] and called upon States to,

> do their utmost to ensure continuity in service provision and to keep offering support and protection to women and girls at risk of violence, with the involvement of all relevant actors: law enforcement agencies, social services, the justice sector, specialist support services and all relevant ministries.

Conclusion

In conclusion therefore, it can be clearly seen that the relevant academic literature contains extensive discussion of the elements which are needed in order to provide an effective criminal justice response to the issue of domestic abuse. Not only must adequate legislation be put in place, but key agencies within the criminal justice system, such as the police, the prosecution service and the courts, must also respond in an effective manner. In addition, human rights bodies at both the UN and regional levels have considered in detail the standards which should be applied in this area. Chapters 3 and 4 will proceed to evaluate the responses of the criminal justice system in Northern Ireland to domestic abuse. Chapter 3 will discuss responses historically, with a particular focus on the period from 2010 until 2019. Chapter 4 will then analyse very current responses, and will focus on 2020–2022.

Notes

1 Discussion of these issues can also be found in McQuigg R.J.A., *International Human Rights Law and Domestic Violence*, 2011, Routledge, Abingdon, at 19–30.
2 Some discussion of these standards can also be found in McQuigg, op. cit., at 79–82.
3 Freedman A.E., 'Symposium: Fact-finding in civil domestic violence cases: Secondary traumatic stress and the need for compassionate witnesses', (2003) 11 *American University Journal of Gender, Social Policy & the Law* 567 at 588.
4 Freedman, op. cit., at 588.
5 James A., 'In practice: Prosecuting domestic violence', (2008) *Family Law* 456.
6 Freedman, op. cit., at 589–590.
7 Freedman, op. cit., at 590–591.
8 Merry S.E., 'Rights talk and the experience of law: Implementing women's human rights to protection from violence', (2003) 25 *Human Rights Quarterly* 343 at 378.
9 Hague G. and Malos E., *Domestic Violence: Action for Change*, 2005, New Clarion Press, Cheltenham, at 108.
10 Mullender A. and Hague G., 'Women Survivors' Views', in J. Taylor-Browne (ed.), *What Works in Reducing Domestic Violence? A Comprehensive Guide for Professionals*, 2001, Whiting & Birch Ltd, London, 1–33 at 20.
11 Mullender and Hague, op. cit., at 21.
12 Mullender and Hague, op. cit., at 21.
13 This issue is also discussed in McQuigg R.J.A., 'Northern Ireland new offence of domestic abuse', (2021) *Statute Law Review* early online access: https://doi.org/10.1093/slr/hmab013
14 [1997] 4 All ER 225.
15 For discussion of the concept of coercive control, see Stark E., *Coercive Control: How Men Trap Women in Personal Life*, 2007, Oxford University Press, Oxford; Stark E., 'Rethinking coercive control', (2009) 15 *Violence Against Women* 1509; Williamson E., 'Living in the world of the domestic violence perpetrator: Negotiating the unreality of coercive control', (2010) 16 *Violence Against Women* 1412; Stark E., 'Looking beyond domestic violence: Policing coercive control', (2012) 12 *Journal of Police Crisis Negotiations* 199; and Stark E. and Hester M., 'Coercive control: Update and review', (2019) 25 *Violence Against Women* 81.
16 Herring J., *Domestic Abuse and Human Rights*, 2020, Intersentia, Cambridge, at 26.
17 Fitz-gibbon K., Walklate S. and McCulloch J., 'Editorial introduction', (2018) 18 *Criminology and Criminal Justice* 3 at 3.
18 Women's Aid, 'What Is Coercive Control?', www.womensaid.org.uk/information-support/what-is-domestic-abuse/coercive-control/

19 Jeffries S., 'In the best interests of the abuser: Coercive control, child custody proceedings and the "expert" assessments that guide judicial determinations', (2016) 5 *Laws* 14 at 15.
20 Herring, op. cit., at 27.
21 Burton M., *Legal Responses to Domestic Violence*, 2008, Routledge, Abingdon, at 66.
22 Burton, op. cit., at 68.
23 Tadros V., 'The Distinctiveness of Domestic Abuse: A Freedom Based Account', in A. Duff and S. Green (eds.), *Defining Crimes*, 2005, Oxford University Press, Oxford, 119–142.
24 Youngs J., 'Domestic violence and the criminal law: Reconceptualising reform', (2015) 79 *Journal of Criminal Law* 55 at 65.
25 Youngs, op. cit., at 66.
26 Tolmie J.R., 'Coercive control: To criminalize or not to criminalize?', (2018) 18 *Criminology and Criminal Justice* 50 at 51–52.
27 Bettinson V. and Bishop C., 'Is the creation of a discrete offence of coercive control necessary to combat domestic violence?', (2015) 66 *Northern Ireland Legal Quarterly* 179 at 196.
28 Youngs, op. cit., at 56. For further discussion of the need for a discrete offence, see McMahon M. and McGorrery P. (eds.) *Criminalising Coercive Control: Family Violence and the Criminal* Law, 2020, Springer, Singapore; Burman M. and Brooks-Hay O., 'Aligning policy and law? The creation of a domestic abuse offence incorporating coercive control', (2018) 18 *Criminology and Criminal Justice* 67; Bettinson V., 'Criminalising coercive control in domestic violence cases: Should Scotland follow the path of England and Wales?', (2016) *Criminal Law Review* 165; Douglas H., 'Do we need a specific domestic violence offence?', (2015) 39 *Melbourne University Law Review* 434; Hanna C., 'The paradox of progress: Translating Evan Stark's coercive control into legal doctrine for abused women', (2009) 15 *Violence Against Women* 1458; and Tuerkheimer D., 'Recognising and remedying the harm of battering: A call to criminalise domestic violence', (2004) 94 *Journal of Criminal Law and Criminology* 959.
29 Stanko E.A, *Intimate Intrusions*, 1985, Routledge, Abingdon, at 10.
30 Armatta J., 'Getting beyond the law's complicity in intimate violence against women', (1997) 33 *Willamette Law Review* 774 at 812.
31 Hague and Malos, op. cit., at 177.
32 Bruce E., 'Attitudes of Social Workers and Police in the Select Committee Report on Violence to Women and Children', in University of Bradford, *Battered Women and Abused Children – Intricacies of Legal and Administrative Intervention* (1979) Issues Publications, University of Bradford, 50–61 at 53.
33 Smith L.J.F., 'Domestic Violence: An Overview of the Literature', 1989, Home Office Research Study 107, HMSO, London, at 47.
34 Smith, op. cit., at 47.
35 Smith, op. cit., at 47.
36 Smith, op. cit., at 55.
37 Armatta, op. cit., at 812.

38 Mullender and Hague, op. cit., at 20.
39 Mullender and Hague, op. cit., at 20.
40 Mullender and Hague, op. cit., at 20.
41 Mullender and Hague, op. cit., at 20.
42 Hanmer J. and Griffiths S., 'Effective Policing', in J. Taylor-Browne (ed.), *What Works in Reducing Domestic Violence? A Comprehensive Guide for Professionals*, 2001, Whiting & Birch Ltd, London, 123–150 at 146.
43 Hanmer and Griffiths, op. cit., at 147.
44 Hanmer and Griffiths, op. cit., at 147.
45 Hague G., Mullender A., Aris R. and Dear W., 'Abused Women's Perspectives: Responsiveness and Accountability of Domestic Violence and Inter-Agency Initiatives', 2001, Report to the ESRC, at 11.
46 Sullivan C.M., 'Using the ESID model to reduce intimate male violence against women', (2003) 32 *American Journal of Community Psychology* 295 at 296.
47 Goodmark L., 'Symposium: Domestic violence & the law: Theory, policy, and practice: Law is the answer? Do we know that for sure?: Questioning the efficacy of legal interventions for battered women', (2004) 23 *Saint Louis University Public Law Review* 7 at 13.
48 Hester M. and Westmarland N., 'Tackling Domestic Violence: Effective Interventions and Approaches', Home Office Research Study 290 (2005) Home Office Research, Development and Statistics Directorate, at 42.
49 Hester and Westmarland, op. cit., at x.
50 Hague and Malos, op. cit., at 77.
51 Hughes B., 'Can domestic violence be considered a violation of human rights law?', (2006) 14 *British Journal of Midwifery* 192.
52 Connelly C. and Cavanagh K., 'Domestic abuse, civil protection orders and the "new criminologies": Is there any value in engaging with the law?', (2007) 15 *Feminist Legal Studies* 259 at 275.
53 Diduck A. and Kaganas F., *Family Law, Gender and the State*, 1999, Hart Publishing, Oxford, at 332.
54 Mullender and Hague, op. cit., at 21.
55 Mullender and Hague, op. cit., at 21.
56 Hanmer and Griffiths, op. cit., at 140.
57 Hanmer and Griffiths, op. cit., at 142.
58 Hanmer and Griffiths, op. cit., at 143.
59 United Nations Centre for Social Development and Humanitarian Affairs, Strategies for Confronting Domestic Violence: A Resource Manual 7 (1993) U.N.Doc.ST/CSDHA/20 (1993) at 38, as quoted by Thomas C., 'Domestic Violence', in K.D. Askin and D.M. Koenig (eds.) *Women and International Human Rights Law* (Vol.1), 1999, Transnational Publishers Inc., New York, 219–256 at 227.
60 Stanko, op. cit., at 130.
61 Stanko, op. cit., at 130.
62 Cretney A. and Davis G., 'Prosecuting 'domestic' assault', (1996) *Criminal Law Review* 162 at 166.

63 Cretney A. and Davis G., 'Prosecuting domestic assault: Victims failing courts, or courts failing victims?', (1997) 36 *The Howard Journal* 146 at 147–149.
64 Cretney and Davis (1997), op. cit., at 154.
65 Cretney and Davis (1997), op. cit., at 147.
66 Thomas, op. cit., at 227.
67 Edwards S., 'New Directions in Prosecution', in J. Taylor-Browne (ed.), *What Works in Reducing Domestic Violence? A Comprehensive Guide for Professionals*, 2001, Whiting & Birch Ltd, London, 211–238 at 223.
68 Edwards, op. cit., at 221.
69 Edwards, op. cit., at 212.
70 Edwards, op. cit., at 212.
71 Miles J., 'Domestic Violence', in J. Herring (ed.), *Family Law – Issues, Debates, Policy*, 2001, Willan Publishing, Devon, 78–124 at 92.
72 Hester M., Hanmer J., Coulson S., Morahan M. and Razak A, *Domestic Violence: Making It Through the Criminal Justice System*, 2003, University of Sunderland and Northern Rock Foundation, Sunderland, at 13.
73 Hester, Hanmer, Coulson, Morahan and Razak, op. cit., at 9.
74 Hester and Westmarland, op. cit., at 43.
75 Hall M., 'The Relationship between victims and prosecutors: Defending victims' rights?', (2010) *Criminal Law Review* 31 at 40.
76 Hague and Malos, op. cit., at 102.
77 Smith, op. cit., at 94.
78 Smith, op. cit., at 95.
79 Berry D.B., *The Domestic Violence Sourcebook*, 1998, Lowell House, Los Angeles, at 154–155.
80 Berry, op. cit., at 154–155.
81 Hester and Westmarland, op. cit., at 56.
82 Thomas, op. cit., at 219.
83 Diduck and Kaganas, op. cit., at 333.
84 Miles, op. cit., at 93.
85 Edwards, op. cit., at 212.
86 Mullender, Hague, Aris and Dear, op. cit., at 13.
87 Hester, Hanmer, Coulson, Morahan and Razak, op. cit., at 13.
88 Hester, Hanmer, Coulson, Morahan and Razak, op. cit., at 13.
89 Fredman S., *Human Rights Transformed – Positive Rights and Positive Duties*, 2009, Oxford University Press, Oxford, at 1. See also Hirschl R., '"Negative" rights vs. "positive" entitlements: A comparative study of judicial interpretations of rights in an emerging neo-liberal economic order', (2000) 22 *Human Rights Quarterly* 1060.
90 Burton, op. cit., 7. See also Lacey N., *Unspeakable Subjects*, 1998, Hart Publishing, Oxford, at 71–97; Romany C., 'Women as aliens: A feminist critique of the public/private distinction in international human rights law' (1993) 6 *Harvard Human Rights Journal* 87; and Cook R.J., 'Women's International Human Rights Law: The Way Forward', in R.J. Cook (ed.),

Human Rights of Women – National and International Perspectives, 1994, University of Pennsylvania Press, Pennsylvania, 3–36 at 3.

91 UN Committee on the Elimination of Discrimination Against Women, General Recommendation No. 19: Violence against women (1992), para. 4.

92 Para. 6.

93 Para. 7.

94 Para. 9.

95 Para. 23.

96 Declaration on the Elimination of Violence Against Women, General Assembly Resolution 48/104 (20 December 1993).

97 Article 3.

98 United Nations, 'Vienna Declaration and Programme of Action' (25 June 1993).

99 Stark B., 'Symposium on integrating responses to domestic violence', (2001) 47 *Loyola Law Review* 255 at 265.

100 Report of the Special Rapporteur on violence against women, its causes and consequences – A framework for model legislation on domestic violence, E/CN.4/1996/53/Add.2 (2 February 1996).

101 Beijing Platform for Action, U.N. Doc.A/CONF.177/20 (1995).

102 See for example, Commission on Human Rights Resolution 2001/49 (23 April 2001); Commission on Human Rights Resolution 2004/46, 20 April 2004; and Human Rights Council Resolution 14/12 (30 June 2010).

103 For further discussion of developments at the UN level, see McQuigg (2011), op. cit., at 78–98; McQuigg R.J.A., *The Istanbul Convention, Domestic Violence and Human* Rights, 2017, Routledge, Abingdon, 22–31; Meyersfeld B., *Domestic Violence and International Law* (2010) Hart Publishing, Oxford, 24–78; and Hesselbacher L., 'State obligations regarding domestic violence: The European Court of Human Rights, due diligence, and international legal minimums of protection', (2010) 8 *Northwestern Journal of International Human Rights* 190 at 191–200.

104 See for example, *AT v Hungary* (Communication No. 2/2003, 26 January 2005, CEDAW/C/32/D/2/2003); *Goekce v Austria* (Communication No. 5/2005, 6 August 2007, CEDAW/C/39/D/5/2005); *Yildirim v Austria* (Communication No. 6/2005, 1 October 2007, CEDAW/C/39/D/6/2005); *VK v Bulgaria* (Communication No. 20/2008, 17 August 2011, CEDAW/C/49/D/20/2008); and *Jallow v Bulgaria* (Communication No. 32/2011, 28 August 2012, CEDAW/C/52/D/32/2011).

105 See for example, *Bevacqua and S. v Bulgaria* (application no. 71127/01, judgment of 12 June 2008); *Opuz v Turkey* (application no. 33401/02, judgment of 9 June 2009); *E.S. and Others v Slovakia* (application no. 8227/04, judgment of 15 September 2009); *A v Croatia* (application no. 55164/08, judgment of 14 October 2010); *Hajduova v Slovakia* (application no. 2660/03, judgment of 30 November 2010); *Kalucza v Hungary* (application no. 57693/10, judgment of 24 April 2012); *Valiuliene v Lithuania* (application no. 33234/07, judgment of 26 March 2013); *Eremia*

and Others v Republic of Moldova (application no. 3564/11, judgment of 28 May 2013); *M.G. v Turkey* (application no. 646/10, judgment of 22 March 2016); *Balsan v Romania* (application no. 49645/09, judgment of 23 May 2017); *Talpis v Italy* (application no. 41237/14, judgment of 18 September 2017); and *Volodina v Russia* (application no. 41261/17, judgment of 9 July 2019).

106 For further discussion of the case law of the European Court of Human Rights on domestic abuse, see McQuigg (2017), op. cit., 60–67; Herring, op. cit., 60–99; Burton M., 'The human rights of victims of domestic violence: *Opuz v Turkey*', (2010) 22 *Child and Family Law Quarterly* 131; McQuigg R.J.A., '*Kurt v Austria*: Applying the *Osman* test to cases of domestic violence', (2020) *European Human Rights Law Review* 394; McQuigg R.J.A., 'Domestic violence as a human rights issue: *Rumor v Italy*', (2015) 26 *European Journal of International Law* 1009; and McQuigg R.J.A., 'The European Court of Human Rights and domestic violence: *Valiuliene v Lithuania*', (2014) 18 *International Journal of Human Rights* 756.

107 For discussion of the Istanbul Convention, see McQuigg (2017), op. cit; McQuigg R.J.A., 'What potential does the Council of Europe Convention on Violence against Women hold as regards domestic violence?', (2012) 16 *International Journal of Human Rights* 947; and McQuigg R.J.A., 'A contextual analysis of the Council of Europe's Convention on Preventing and Combating Violence Against Women', (2012) 1 *International Human Rights Law Review* 367.

108 Report of the World Conference of the United Nations Decade for Women: Equality, Development and Peace, Copenhagen, July 1980, U.N. Doc A/CONF. 94/35 (80.IV.3), para. 65.

109 General Assembly Resolution 40/36 (1985), para. 7.

110 Report of the World Conference to Review and Appraise the Achievements of the United Nations Decade for Women: Equality, Development and Peace, held in Nairobi, July 1985, including Nairobi Forward-Looking Strategies for the Advancement of Women, U.N. Doc A/CONF.116/28/Rev.1 (85.IV.10), para. 76.

111 General Assembly Resolution 45/114 (1990), para. 2.

112 Para. 24(r)(i).

113 Para. 24(b).

114 Committee on the Elimination of Discrimination Against Women, General Recommendation No. 19: Violence Against Women (1992), para. 6.

115 General Assembly Resolution 48/104 (1993), Article 4(d).

116 Article 4(f).

117 Beijing Platform for Action, U.N. Doc.A/CONF.177/20 (1995), para. 124(b).

118 Para. 124(c).

119 Para. 124(d).

120 Para. 124(g).

121 Para. 124(h).

122 Para. 124(l).
123 Report of the Special Rapporteur on violence against women, its causes and consequences – A framework for model legislation on domestic violence, E/CN.4/1996/53/Add.2, 2 February 1996, para. 12.
124 Para. 13.
125 Para. 14.
126 Para. 16.
127 Para. 17(a).
128 Para. 17(b).
129 Para. 17(c).
130 Para. 17(e).
131 Para. 17(f).
132 Para. 17(h).
133 Para. 21(e).
134 Para. 21(d).
135 Para. 23.
136 Para. 24.
137 Para. 45.
138 Para. 49.
139 Para. 55.
140 Para. 54.
141 Commission on Human Rights Resolution 2001/49, para. 10(c).
142 Commission on Human Rights Resolution 2004/46, para. 15.
143 Para. 15(g).
144 Para. 15(h).
145 UN General Assembly Resolution 58/147, para. 5.
146 Para. 6.
147 Para. 7(a).
148 Para. 7(c).
149 Para. 7(f).
150 Para. 7(g).
151 Para. 7(h).
152 Para. 7(i).
153 General Assembly Resolution 61/143 (2006), para. 7.
154 Para. 8(i).
155 UN Committee on the Elimination of Discrimination Against Women, General Recommendation No. 35: Gender-based Violence against Women (1992).
156 For further discussion of General Recommendation 35, see McQuigg R.J.A., 'The CEDAW Committee and gender-based violence against women: General Recommendation No 35', (2017) 6 *International Human Rights Law Review* 263.
157 Para. 26(a).
158 Para. 29.
159 Para. 30.
160 Para. 44.

161 Para. 26(c).
162 Para. 40(a).
163 Para. 40(c).
164 Para. 41.
165 Romania deposited such a reservation on 23 May 2016. For a full list of the reservations and declarations made by States Parties to the Istanbul Convention, see www.coe.int/en/web/conventions/full-list/-/conventions/treaty/210/declarations?p_auth=VHYoKh1z
166 Istanbul Convention, Article 46(a).
167 Article 46(b).
168 Article 46(c).
169 Article 46(d).
170 Article 46(f).
171 Article 46(g).
172 Article 46(h).
173 Article 46(i).
174 Council of Europe, 'Explanatory Report to Council of Europe Convention on Preventing and Combating Violence Against Women and Domestic Violence', para. 256.
175 Para. 260.
176 See further McQuigg (2011), op. cit., at 25 and 98.
177 Council of Europe, 'Explanatory Report to Council of Europe Convention on Preventing and Combating Violence Against Women and Domestic Violence', para. 282.
178 Istanbul Convention, Article 56(1)(b).
179 Article 56(1)(c).
180 Article 56(1)(d).
181 Article 56(1)(g).
182 Article 56(1)(i).
183 Maputo Protocol, Article 4(2)(a).
184 Article 4(2)(b).
185 Article 4(2)(e).
186 Article 2(1) states that, 'Everyone's right to life shall be protected by law'.
187 Article 3 states that, 'No one shall be subjected to torture or to inhuman or degrading treatment or punishment'.
188 Article 8(1) states that, 'Everyone has the right to respect for his private and family life, his home and his correspondence'.
189 The relevant part of Article 14 states that, 'The enjoyment of the rights and freedoms set forth in this Convention shall be secured without discrimination on any ground such as sex …'.
190 Application no. 41261/17, judgment of 9 July 2019, para. 75. For further discussion of *Volodina v Russia*, see McQuigg R.J.A. 'The European Court of Human Rights and domestic violence: *Volodina v. Russia*', (2021) *International Human Rights Law Review* 155.
191 Application no. 62903/15, judgment of 15 June 2021.
192 Application no. 87/1997/871/1083, judgment of 28 October 1998.

193 Para. 116.
194 Para. 116.
195 Para. 116.
196 Application No. 62903/15, judgment of 4 July 2019, Concurring Opinion of Judge Huseynov, para. 3.
197 Concurring Opinion of Judge Huseynov, para. 4.
198 Application number 33234/07, judgment of 26 March 2013. For detailed discussion of this case, see McQuigg (2014), op. cit.
199 Concurring Opinion of Judge Pinto De Albuquerque, para. 31.
200 Application no. 41261/17, judgment of 9 July 2019.
201 Separate Opinion of Judge Pinto De Albuquerque, joined by Judge Dedov, para. 12.
202 Application no. 62903/15, judgment of 15 June 2021, para. 164.
203 Para. 165.
204 Para. 166.
205 Para. 168.
206 Para. 169.
207 Para. 173.
208 Para. 175.
209 Para. 175.
210 Para. 168. For further discussion of *Kurt v Austria*, see McQuigg (2020), op. cit.; and McQuigg R.J.A., '*Kurt v Austria*: Domestic violence before the Grand Chamber of the European Court of Human Rights', (2021) *European Human Rights Law Review* 550.
211 UN Women, 'COVID-19 and Ending Violence Against Women and Girls', www.unwomen.org/-/media/headquarters/attachments/sections/library/publications/2020/issue-brief-covid-19-and-ending-violence-against-women-and-girls-en.pdf?la=en&vs=5006
212 UN Special Rapporteur on violence against women, its causes and consequences, 'States must combat domestic violence in the context of Covid-19 lockdowns', 27 March 2020, www.ohchr.org/EN/NewsEvents/Pages/DisplayNews.aspx?NewsID=25749&LangID=E
213 Para. 3.
214 Para. 3.
215 Council of Europe, '"For many women and children, the home is not a safe place". Statement by the President of GREVIO, Marceline Naudi, on the need to uphold the standards of the Istanbul Convention in times of a pandemic', 24 March 2020, https://rm.coe.int/grevio-statement-covid-24-march-2020/pdfa/16809cf55e

3 Criminal Justice Responses to Domestic Abuse in Northern Ireland Pre-2020

This chapter analyses the responses of the criminal justice system in Northern Ireland to domestic abuse prior to 2020. Political violence was a part of life in Northern Ireland for around 30 years from the late 1960s until the late 1990s, and the 'Troubles' certainly impacted upon responses to domestic abuse during this time. However, the focus of the chapter is on analysing much more recent responses of the criminal justice system to domestic abuse, specifically during the decade from around 2010 until 2019. During this decade, several reports were issued by Criminal Justice Inspection Northern Ireland (CJINI) which focused on the responses of the criminal justice system to domestic abuse,[1] and these reports are discussed in this chapter. The Department of Justice's 2016 public consultation on domestic abuse[2] and the subsequent creation of a domestic violence disclosure scheme are considered, as is the Department's public consultation of 2018 on responding to stalking.[3] It will be seen that by 2019 the response of the criminal justice system in Northern Ireland to domestic abuse had developed greatly. Nevertheless, problems still remained, particularly as regards the lack of legislation criminalising coercive control.

The Impact of the 'Troubles' on Criminal Justice Responses to Domestic Abuse in Northern Ireland

In the UK context, Burton comments that, 'Until the 1970s there was little recognition of domestic violence as an issue that ought to be tackled by the legal system'.[4] Domestic abuse only emerged as a social problem in the 1970s, and up until that time, was hardly viewed as being a legal issue at all. Even after such abuse began to be recognised as an issue which should be addressed by the criminal justice system, significant problems remained regarding the responses of key agencies, such as the police, prosecutors and the courts, as was discussed in Chapter 2.

DOI: 10.4324/9781003261650-3

These difficulties were exacerbated in the context of Northern Ireland, where the 'Troubles' were very much a part of life from around the late 1960s until the late 1990s. As McWilliams and Ní Aoláin explain, during this time, police resources were almost entirely focused on combating paramilitary activity. Little attention was therefore paid by the criminal justice system to issues such as domestic abuse.[5]

However, the Good Friday Agreement (or Belfast Agreement) was signed on 10 April 1998.[6] This Agreement formed the basis for Northern Ireland's current devolved system of government; and covered the creation of an Assembly, a North/South Ministerial Council, a British-Irish Council and a British-Irish Governmental Conference. A referendum on the Agreement was held on 22 May 1998, and 71.1 per cent of those voting in Northern Ireland were in favour of its acceptance. The Northern Ireland Act 1998 was subsequently enacted in order to implement the Agreement. This Act set out the powers of the Assembly and the Executive as regards transferred, excepted and reserved matters. The Good Friday Agreement brought an end to a large amount, although not all, of Northern Ireland's political violence; however the suffering of victims of abuse taking place within their own homes continued.

Criminal Justice Inspection Northern Ireland Report – December 2010

The Good Friday Agreement provided for a 'wide ranging review of criminal justice…to be carried out by the British Government through a mechanism with an independent element, in consultation with the political parties and others'.[7] The subsequent Criminal Justice Review, which reported in 2000, highlighted the importance of inspection as a tool for holding criminal justice agencies to account, and CJINI was subsequently established as a single, independent criminal justice inspectorate.[8]

In December 2010, CJINI issued a report on the handling of domestic violence and abuse cases by the criminal justice system in Northern Ireland.[9] A 'Tackling Violence at Home' regional strategy had been launched in 2005 by the Northern Ireland Office and the Department of Health, Social Services and Public Safety.[10] CJINI highlighted that improvements had been made in the way in which the criminal justice system dealt with cases of domestic abuse, and that developments had been made to improve processes and ways of working. These included the specialisation of investigators and prosecutors, greater levels of engagement with the community and voluntary sector, and the rolling out of the Multi-Agency Risk Assessment Conference (MARAC) process. However, improvements were still necessary in order to provide greater support for victims, and to bring the approach in Northern Ireland into line with other jurisdictions.[11]

The agencies involved in investigating and prosecuting cases of domestic abuse had developed procedures and policies which set out appropriate standards and methods for dealing with these types of cases. CJINI found that the Police Service of Northern Ireland (PSNI) generally adhered to these in operational practice although variations existed in their implementation across the districts. The quality of information provided to officers responding to domestic abuse calls varied and CJINI commented that a checklist should be developed to improve this. Domestic Abuse Officers were located within Public Protection Units in each district and generally dealt with investigations involving repeat offenders or more serious offences. The training of new recruits and specialist officers had been developed and a risk assessment tool was about to be rolled out to assist in identifying high-risk victims. Although feedback on the quality of evidence obtained by police officers was mixed, CJINI were of the view that use of digital photographic equipment and the consideration of the roll out of a Body Worn Digital Recording System should improve this. The requirements for officers when attending incidents involving domestic abuse were set out in PSNI policies, and CJINI commented that it was imperative that supervisors monitored adherence to these requirements in a proactive manner. According to CJINI, greater clarity was needed regarding the role and training required for Domestic Abuse Officers.[12]

The PSNI had been proactive in their role in the MARAC pilot and had been preparing for its roll out. In addition, the PSNI had also been involved in two pilot projects with Women's Aid involving the co-location of a support worker with the Domestic Abuse Team. Inspectors heard that improvements had been made in taking withdrawal statements and that processes had been put in place in order to ensure follow-up by Domestic Abuse Officers in relation to repeat or serious offences. However, whilst good practice existed regarding the response to and investigation of domestic abuse, there nevertheless appeared to be a lack of consistency in the way in which victims were dealt with, which could depend upon where the offence occurred.[13]

As regards the Public Prosecution Service (PPS), domestic abuse specialists had been appointed but the role was still at an early stage. Although all public prosecutors were expected to prosecute the large number of cases with a domestic motivation which were received from the PSNI, over half of such cases were directed for no prosecution. High numbers of victims withdrew their support for the prosecution, and in such instances the PPS had to direct no prosecution due to a lack of evidence. CJINI were of the view that:

> The assessment of risk and decisions around taking a prosecution where the victim had withdrawn their support was a considerable challenge for prosecutors and agreement need(ed) to be reached to obtain higher quality information from the PSNI to assist in this.[14]

Issues had also been raised in relation to the performance of prosecutors at court. The views of victims on the police and prosecutorial processes varied, and feelings of apprehension were common when updates on the progress of the case were not received. Nevertheless,

> Inspectors met a great number of committed and motivated individuals both inside and outside the criminal justice system during the course of the inspection, who described the genuine efforts they had made and continued to make to provide a better service for victims of domestic violence and abuse'.[15]

CJINI proceeded to make 13 recommendations as to improvements which should be made to the response of the criminal justice system in Northern Ireland to domestic abuse. These recommendations included that the PSNI should ensure the taking place of proactive monitoring by supervisors to ensure consistency of approach, particularly in reviewing decisions not to arrest. Also, in cases of serious crime, supervisors should take an active role from the outset in order to ensure a consistent and effective investigation.[16] CJINI recommended that consideration should be given by legislators of the enactment of provisions which would enable the PSNI to issue a Domestic Violence Protection Order of up to 14 days duration, to prevent a suspected perpetrator from entering the address of the victim and/or prevent contact by the suspected perpetrator with the victim.[17] The PSNI should review the role of and skill set requirements for Domestic Abuse Officers and Public Protection Unit supervisors.[18] According to CJINI, the PPS should continue to review domestic abuse files where a decision not to prosecute had been made in order to ascertain whether actions could be taken to improve the likelihood of the test for prosecution being met.[19] The PSNI and the PPS should also reach agreement regarding the inclusion of assessments by investigating officers of the reasons for withdrawal statements being made, and views in relation to whether and, if appropriate, how the case should proceed to prosecution without the consent of the victim.[20] In addition, the Management Board of the PPS should continue to ensure that there was effective and regular monitoring of the performance of prosecutors in the Magistrates' Courts, and that prompt feedback was given to prosecutors and any training needs addressed.[21]

CJINI also recommended that the Protection and Justice sub-group of the 'Tackling Violence at Home' Regional Steering Group should assess the feasibility of developing a Specialist Domestic Violence Court in Northern Ireland.[22] The Department of Justice should, as a matter of urgency, develop plans for a properly resourced Independent Domestic Violence Advisor service to provide support and advocacy for victims of domestic abuse to complement the roll out of the MARAC process.[23]

In addition, CJINI recommended that the PSNI develop a call taker checklist in order to enable call handlers to support the victim and gather evidence.[24] The PSNI, in consultation with the PPS, should introduce digital photographic equipment to be made available to response officers for use in domestic abuse offences, with the aim of enhancing the evidence available for the case file submitted to the PPS.[25] The PSNI should also explore the feasibility of further rollout of the Body Worn Digital Recording System,[26] and should investigate, in conjunction with Women's Aid, the possibility of further co-location of support workers with Public Protection Units.[27] In addition, CJINI recommended that the PPS should develop additional ways of seeking confirmation of the attendance at court of all victims of domestic abuse prior to the trial date, and ensure that consideration is given as to potential alternative courses of action where it is believed the victim may not attend court.[28]

Criminal Justice Inspection Northern Ireland Follow-Up Report – October 2013

In October 2013, CJINI published a report the purpose of which was to assess the progress which had been made against each of the recommendations which had been made in 2010.[29] Overall, it was concluded that of the 13 recommendations which had been made, only one of these had been achieved, with six recommendations having been partially achieved and the remaining six not achieved.

The recommendation which CJINI assessed as having been achieved was that the PPS should continue to review domestic abuse files where a decision not to prosecute had been made in order to ascertain whether actions could be taken to improve the likelihood of the test for prosecution being met. CJINI inspectors were satisfied that the PPS was placing a focus on domestic abuse offences in terms of quality assuring the decision-making process of prosecutors. CJINI found positive examples of partnership working between the PSNI and the PPS, and prosecutors who had been appointed as Domestic Violence Specialists confirmed that other prosecutors approached them to ask for advice regarding difficult cases. Also, representatives from Women's Aid confirmed that they had seen an improvement in terms of decisions regarding the taking forward of cases.[30]

The recommendations which were assessed as having been partially achieved included that the PSNI should ensure proactive monitoring by supervisors to ensure consistency of approach, particularly in reviewing decisions not to arrest; and that in cases of serious crime, supervisors should take an active role from the outset in order to ensure a consistent and effective investigation. Domestic Abuse Officers reported 'a mixed picture in terms of proactivity of Officers across the police Districts, with differences in approach noted depending on which response section was responding to calls'.[31] However, serious crime incidents were highlighted as being investigated more effectively. The use of Domestic Abuse, Stalking and Harassment (DASH) risk assessment forms was also referred to as being better in some areas than others. The CJINI report stated that, 'There is therefore still a need for the PSNI to continue to strive for a more consistent approach across police Districts when dealing with domestic violence and abuse incidents', and that, 'A solution to fully address the inconsistencies in practice in relation to domestic violence and abuse (was) therefore some way off at the time of this follow-up review'.[32]

Another recommendation which CJINI assessed as having been partially achieved was that the PPS and PSNI should reach agreement regarding the inclusion of assessments by investigating officers of the reasons for withdrawal statements being made and views in relation to whether and, if appropriate, how the case should proceed to prosecution without the consent of the victim. A PSNI Policy Directive on 'Police Response to Domestic Incidents' stated that any retraction statement should, where possible, be recorded by a Domestic Abuse Officer, and that such a statement should include, for example, confirmation of whether the original statement given to police was true, reasons for withdrawing the allegation, and whether the victim had been put under any pressure to withdraw. In addition, the Service Level Agreement between the PSNI and the PPS included a section on withdrawal of complaints in domestic abuse cases, which also set out the issues to be included in withdrawal statements. The Service Level Agreement specified that the officer taking the statement should inform the PPS of their views on the truthfulness of the reasons given by the victim; safety matters regarding the victim and any children; how the victim would be likely to react to being compelled; and their recommendation in relation to how the case should be dealt with. However, both the police and prosecutors indicated to CJINI that the quality of the withdrawal statement tended to differ depending on whether or not it had been taken by a Domestic Abuse Officer. It was highlighted that one police district had a policy under which only Domestic Abuse Officers could take withdrawal statements, and that this policy led to fewer victims withdrawing due to Domestic Violence Officers being more skilled in explaining the risks of withdrawing and the benefits of continuing with the criminal justice process. The CJINI report concluded that, whilst the Policy Directive and the Service Level Agreement set out the required content of withdrawal statements, it seemed that there was still work to be done to ensure this was implemented in practice.[33]

The recommendation that the Management Board of the PPS should continue to ensure that there was effective and regular monitoring of the performance of prosecutors in the Magistrates' Courts, and that prompt feedback was given to prosecutors and any training needs addressed, was also assessed by CJINI inspectors as having been partially achieved. It was found that although the PPS were continuing to develop their approach to the monitoring of performance in relation to advocacy, and that intense training had been provided, work was still needed in order to ensure the implementation of this training into practice, and in relation to monitoring and giving feedback to prosecutors on an ongoing basis.[34]

The fourth recommendation which the CJINI inspectors deemed to be partially achieved was that which related to the Protection and Justice sub-group of the 'Tackling Violence at Home' Regional Steering Group assessing the feasibility of developing a Specialist Domestic Violence Court in Northern Ireland. Although further work was still needed in relation to this recommendation, the CJINI report highlighted the court listing arrangement in Derry/Londonderry which had begun in November 2011 and which involved criminal cases involving domestic abuse being listed on a set day each month. There was an onus on the PPS to identify the cases to be included in this listing, but anecdotal evidence suggested that this system was working effectively. One prosecutor then dealt with all of the cases on the day of the court. Some victims attending court were supported by Women's Aid, and it seemed that the number of victims attending court had increased. Overall, those involved with this listing arrangement felt that it was a positive approach. A formal evaluation was anticipated which would be provided to the judiciary to inform their consideration of the roll out of these arrangements.[35]

The recommendation that the PSNI should investigate, in conjunction with Women's Aid, the possibility of further co-location of support workers with Public Protection Units was also assessed by the CJINI inspectors as having been partially achieved. At the time of the report, there were Women's Aid support workers co-located with two Public Protection Units and a further two Units had dedicated workers based out of station. However, there was no corporate approach to this issue, and decisions around whether to fund these posts were left to individual District Commanders. A Service Level Agreement for all co-located workers was being developed by the PSNI with Women's Aid groups in order to ensure consistency of service delivery for victims.[36]

The final recommendation which CJINI found to be partially achieved was that the PPS should develop additional ways of seeking confirmation of the attendance at court of all victims of domestic abuse prior to the trial date, and ensure that consideration was given as to potential alternative courses of action where it was believed the victim may not attend court. A Victim and Witness Care Unit was being piloted by the PSNI and the PPS, and in locations in which this Unit had been implemented, victims would be asked during initial contact how they would prefer to be contacted, such as by letter, by telephone call or by a text message. However, in locations in which this Unit had not yet been implemented, although the follow-up by Community Liaison Teams to unanswered letters had improved, there were still issues in some areas. Better awareness of the likelihood of the victim attending court should allow prosecutors to develop alternative courses of action where it was believed the victim may not attend. The CJINI report concluded that it was still too early to assess the full impact of the measures which had been taken, but that it was evident that improvements were being made.[37]

However, there were also six recommendations from the 2010 report which CJINI deemed not to have been achieved. The first of these was that consideration should be given by legislators of the enactment of provisions which would enable the PSNI to issue a Domestic Violence Protection Order of up to 14 days duration, to prevent a suspected perpetrator from entering the address of the victim and/or prevent contact by the suspected perpetrator with the victim. At the time of the 2013 follow-up report, the Home Office was piloting Domestic Violence Protection Orders in the Greater Manchester, Wiltshire and West Mercia police areas. The Department of Justice had therefore decided to await the outcome of this pilot before making decisions regarding the introduction of Domestic Violence Protection Orders in Northern Ireland, in order to enable the identification of any lessons learnt and the avoidance of repeating any mistakes made. This approach was certainly understandable, however the recommendation in question was nevertheless assessed as not having been achieved.[38]

The second recommendation which was deemed not to have been achieved was that the PSNI should review the role of and skill set requirements for Domestic Abuse Officers and Public Protection Unit supervisors. The CJINI inspectors found that the work which was required to progress this recommendation had been stalled due to a wider review of operational policing in districts which included Public Protection Units, thus resulting in the recommendation not having been achieved.[39]

The third recommendation which had not been achieved was that plans should be developed for a properly resourced Independent Domestic Violence Advisor service to provide support and advocacy for victims of domestic abuse to complement the roll out of the MARAC process. Due to funding issues, it had been decided that a full Independent Domestic Violence Advisor service, such as that which was available in England and Wales, would not be initially implemented. Instead, the Department of Justice had decided to seek a supplier for a service that would support high risk victims through the MARAC and whilst a safety plan was developed and implemented. It was however unlikely that the victim would be supported through any criminal justice process, although they would hopefully have been signposted to organisations such as Women's Aid who could provide further assistance. In response, the CJINI inspectors remained concerned regarding the implementation of an Independent Domestic Violence Advisor service which was not sufficiently resourced to meet the full range of needs of all high-risk victims.[40]

The fourth recommendation which the CJINI inspectors found had not been achieved was that the PSNI develop a call taker checklist in order to enable call handlers to support victims and gather evidence. Although a call taker checklist had been developed, this had not yet been implemented and rolled out. Issues frequently arose in relation to the appropriate identification of incidents as being of a domestic nature. CJINI therefore concluded that this recommendation could not yet be considered as having been achieved.[41]

The fifth recommendation which had not been achieved was that the PSNI, in consultation with the PPS, should introduce digital photographic equipment to be made available to response officers for use in domestic abuse offences, with the aim of enhancing the evidence available for the case file submitted to the PPS. Domestic Abuse Officers reported that although photographs were sometimes available, there could be issues with quality and with the technology aspects, such as with uploading them onto the system. Prosecutors also reported that some photographs were received, but that these tended to be of injuries sustained rather than of the scene, and issues were raised regarding the quality of the photographs. Due to the limited use of such photographs, CJINI considered this recommendation as not having been implemented.[42]

The final recommendation which was deemed by the CJINI inspectors as not having been achieved was that the PSNI should explore the feasibility of further rollout of the Body Worn Digital Recording System. However, inspectors were not told of any examples of where body-worn video had been used in domestic abuse cases. The inspectors were advised that until national guidance was forthcoming in relation to, for example, the processing and storage of evidence, the PSNI had placed their decisions surrounding this on hold, and there were thus no plans to roll out the use of such video recording any further at that time.[43]

The 2013 follow-up report concluded that, since the 2010 inspection, the criminal justice agencies were 'working more effectively together and integrating the support of the voluntary and community sector organisations into supporting victims'.[44] However there was still a need to address ongoing issues surrounding the role of Domestic Abuse Officers within the PSNI. The follow-up report stated that:

> Inspectors were disappointed that issues such as this and the collection of evidence via photographs or video recording, had not progressed since the original inspection and that inconsistencies in practice across police Districts were still evident, particularly in light of the challenges faced in helping victims remain engaged with the criminal justice process.[45]

The follow-up report also concluded that there was,

> a need to continue to focus on the reasons why cases drop out of the criminal justice process at all stages, in order to increase the number of cases which ultimately, result in a conviction in court and to ensure that vulnerable victims are supported both in the initial days after the abuse is reported and over the longer term.[46]

In addition, there was 'a need for a particular focus on the victim in these types of cases due to the high numbers who withdraw from the process, particularly those who are high risk'.[47]

Stopping Domestic and Sexual Violence and Abuse in Northern Ireland: A Seven Year Strategy

In March 2016, the Department of Health, Social Services and Public Safety and the Department of Justice issued a seven-year strategy on 'Stopping Domestic and Sexual Violence and Abuse in Northern Ireland'.[48] Part of this strategy focused on continually improving the protection and justice available to victims of abuse and their families. The strategy stated that in this regard, the identified priorities included that, 'Focused protection, support and information will be available for all victims throughout their engagement with the Justice System'. In addition, 'Ongoing assessment of the capacity of the Justice System to respond to current, new and emerging issues will be undertaken in relation to both the protection of victims, and in responding to harmful and violent behaviour'. Also prioritised was the need to, 'Continue to develop and deliver practices and interventions, based on best practice, to effectively address harmful, violent and abusive behaviour'.[49]

The Need for Criminal Legislation on Domestic Abuse

As was mentioned in Chapter 2, prior to the passing of the Domestic Abuse and Civil Proceedings Act (Northern Ireland) 2021, the legislative position as regards domestic abuse in Northern Ireland was problematic. Essentially, there was no specific offence of domestic abuse in this jurisdiction. Instead, incidents of domestic abuse had to be prosecuted under general criminal law statutes such as the Offences Against the Person Act 1861. This was relatively unproblematic in relation to incidents of physical violence, as these could be prosecuted under the 1861 Act as, for instance, common assault under section 42, aggravated assault under section 43, assault occasioning actual bodily harm under section 47, assault occasioning grievous bodily harm under section 18, or unlawful wounding under section 20. In *R v Ireland*; *R v Burstow*[50] it was held that a recognisable psychiatric illness could constitute 'bodily harm' for the purposes of sections 18, 20 and 47 of the Offences Against the Person Act. However, states of mind which are not supported by medical evidence of psychiatric injury are not encompassed by the 1861 Act. This proved to be problematic in a number of cases involving domestic abuse.[51]

For example, in *R v D*[52] the husband of a victim of domestic abuse who had committed suicide was prosecuted for unlawful act manslaughter. In order for the defendant to be convicted, the prosecution needed to establish that there had been an unlawful and dangerous act. The prosecution's case was that the defendant had inflicted serious psychological injury contrary to section 20 of the Offences Against the Person Act, through repeated psychological abuse and some physical violence. However, two of the three psychiatric experts who were consulted by the prosecution, whilst being of the view that the deceased had experienced psychological symptoms as a consequence of the domestic abuse, were unable to conclude that she had suffered from an identifiable psychiatric condition. It was held that the scope of 'bodily harm' was limited to recognisable psychiatric illness, and thus the defendant was acquitted.[53] Prosecuting cases of psychological abuse using the 1861 Act was therefore problematic, and this remained the position in Northern Ireland until the enactment of the 2021 legislation.

As was discussed in Chapter 2, in recent times it has been recognised that domestic abuse encompasses not only physical violence but also the wider concept of 'coercive control'.[54] Many commentators are of the view that there is a need for States to enact specific legislation criminalising such behaviour.[55] Due to such considerations, coercive and controlling behaviour was criminalised in England and Wales under section 76 of the Serious Crime Act 2015;[56] abusive behaviour (including psychological abuse) towards a partner or ex-partner was criminalised in Scotland under section 1 of the Domestic Abuse (Scotland) Act 2018;[57] and coercive control was criminalised in the Republic of Ireland under section 39 of the Domestic Violence Act 2018.

As was also considered in Chapter 2, the necessity for the criminalisation of psychological abuse has been recognised in regional and international human rights standards. For example, Article 33 of the Istanbul Convention states that, 'Parties shall take the necessary legislative or other measures to ensure that the intentional conduct of seriously impairing a person's psychological integrity through coercion or threats is criminalised'. In addition, in *Volodina v Russia*,[58] the European Court of Human Rights recognised that the feelings of anxiety, fear and powerlessness which are caused by coercive and controlling behaviour can amount to inhuman treatment under Article 3 of the ECHR,[59] and in its General Recommendation No. 19 the CEDAW Committee recognised that 'coercion' can amount to gender-based violence.[60] The fact that coercive control was not criminalised in Northern Ireland clearly fell short of human rights standards, and indeed in its 2019 Concluding Observations on the UK's eighth periodic report, the CEDAW Committee expressed concern regarding the legislative position in relation to gender-based violence in Northern Ireland and recommended that the UK, 'Adopt legislative and comprehensive policy measures to protect women from all forms of gender-based violence throughout the State party's jurisdiction, including Northern Ireland'.[61]

In February 2016 the Department of Justice launched a public consultation on domestic abuse which included the question of whether a specific offence capturing coercive and controlling behaviour should be enacted.[62] Overwhelmingly, respondents were of the view that the current criminal law needed to change in order to recognise domestic abuse in all its forms. It was believed that, 'Creating an offence would be a positive step towards ensuring that certain types of abuse are not overlooked or treated less seriously', and it was suggested that the offence should encompass mental, emotional and financial control.[63] Respondents highlighted the fact that the criminal justice system treated and, where appropriate, prosecuted each occurrence of domestic abuse as an individual incident, which meant that the cumulative effect of coercive and controlling behaviour was overlooked. The failure to take the repetition of such acts into consideration meant that the criminal law did not provide effective protection for victims.[64] Respondents also said that perpetrators who used coercive control may seek to justify their behaviour on the ground that it was non-violent. It was therefore noted that as well as providing better protection for victims, a domestic abuse offence would send out a strong message to perpetrators, that all forms of abuse are unacceptable and would have serious consequences.[65] In addition, a number of respondents highlighted the need for a strong sentencing regime that reflected the seriousness of domestic abuse.[66] Some respondents also expressed concerns that prosecuting cases of coercive and controlling behaviour could be difficult, particularly in relation to the gathering of sufficient evidence, and it was thus suggested that innovative approaches to evidence gathering should be considered.[67] It was noted that an offence should encapsulate situations in which ex-partners were continuing to exert coercive and controlling behaviour, even following separation.[68] Legislation criminalising coercive control was subsequently drafted for Northern Ireland, however the passage of this stalled due to the suspension of the Northern Ireland Assembly from January 2017 until January 2020.[69] This meant that, until March 2021, Northern Ireland remained the only jurisdiction within the UK and Ireland in which coercive control was not criminalised.

Domestic Violence and Abuse Disclosure Scheme

The Department of Justice's 2016 consultation on domestic abuse also encompassed the issue of whether a domestic violence disclosure scheme should be developed and implemented in Northern Ireland.

The Department sought views on whether the existing legal provisions surrounding the disclosure of information to an individual (referred to in the consultation as 'A') regarding previous violent offences committed by another individual (referred to in the consultation as 'B') who has an intimate relationship with 'A' are sufficient, or whether the protection available to 'A' should be extended by the establishment of a domestic violence disclosure scheme encompassing consistent processes for the PSNI to consider the disclosure of information to 'A'.[70] The consultation sought views on whether any such disclosure should be facilitated through a 'Right to Ask' scheme, a 'Right to Know' scheme or both. A 'Right to Ask' scheme would involve 'A' having the right to ask the PSNI for a disclosure of information about 'B's' past in a situation in which she has concerns regarding 'B's' behaviour. The decision as to whether information should be disclosed would then be made by a panel. A 'Right to Know' scheme would involve information regarding 'B's' history being proactively disclosed by the PSNI in certain circumstances to 'A'. Again, the decision on whether information should be disclosed would be made by a panel. In addition, the consultation sought views on whether disclosures could be made to a third party such as a sibling or a friend.

Those responding to the consultation were broadly in support of the introduction of both a 'Right to Know' scheme and a 'Right to Ask' scheme 'which fundamentally would formalise the rights of individuals to make timely and informed choices about their relationships'.[71] A number of respondents highlighted issues which would necessitate further consideration in order to ensure the effectiveness of the proposed schemes. For example, the need for safety measures and support provision to be made part of the disclosure process was emphasised. Essentially, victims should have access to assistance and support from the initial point of enquiry to the end of the process and irrespective of whether disclosure was eventually made and of whether 'A' chooses to stay in the relationship.[72] Respondents also referred to the importance of the environment and the manner in which a disclosure would be made, particularly if a disclosure had not been requested.[73]

There was also broad support for the proposal to facilitate a third party being able to request information as often family and friends may see patterns of abuse before 'A' seeks help. The necessity of ensuring the regulation of third party disclosures was highlighted.[74] Respondents broadly welcomed the proposal for a multi-agency panel to be established to determine whether a disclosure should be made.[75] Views on the type of information which should be disclosed under the schemes varied, with a number of respondents indicating that any information pertaining to a history of violence or previous police involvement in relationship issues should be disclosable, whilst others took the view that only domestic abuse incidents should be disclosed.[76] On the question of whether disclosure should extend beyond convictions, some respondents were of the view that intelligence should also be disclosed, particularly as the large majority of domestic abuse does not result in a conviction.[77] However, other respondents referred to potential problems which could arise in relation to the disclosure of intelligence which included issues such as what precisely would constitute intelligence, the veracity of the intelligence sources and the potential for legal challenges. It was therefore suggested that any decision to make a disclosure based on intelligence would have to be subject to robust analysis by the panel.[78]

A Domestic Violence and Abuse Disclosure Scheme (DVADS) was subsequently implemented and commenced in March 2018. This scheme provides individuals with the 'Right to Ask' the PSNI to check if their partner, or the partner of someone they know, has a history of domestic abuse; as well as affording the PSNI the 'Power to Tell' an individual about their partner's abusive history. The 'Right to Ask' is triggered when a member of the public makes an application to the PSNI for information regarding an individual whom they suspect may have a history of abusive behaviour towards a previous partner and where there are concerns in relation to that individual's current behaviour. The 'Power to Tell' is triggered when the PSNI receive indirect information or intelligence regarding a person thought to be at risk from a partner, and where, after appropriate checks are made, the PSNI are of the view that a disclosure should be made to safeguard that person. The guidance issued by the Department of Justice on the scheme states that, 'Critical to the success of the scheme is the need to assess risk at each stage of the disclosure process, as this will help inform the practical actions necessary to safeguard the potential victim, and inform the development of a potential disclosure',[79] and that 'A key element of the disclosure scheme is ensuring that potential or actual victims of domestic violence and abuse are protected from harm'.[80] In addition, the guidance asserts that,

> Protection should also be afforded to any previous victim or a third party making an application that may be identified at risk, as a direct consequence of the scheme. By making a request for disclosure, a person will often also be registering their concerns about possible risks to their own safety, or that of another individual. It is, therefore, essential to this process that police work closely with the local Multi-Agency Risk Assessment Conference (MARAC),

to ensure that any possible risks of harm to the potential victim are fully assessed and managed.[81]

In March 2019, it was reported that over 326 applications had been made to the DVADS during its first year of operation, resulting in 40 people being advised regarding the abusive past of their partners.[82]

Responding to Stalking

In recent times stalking has been recognised as a form of domestic abuse. Indeed, analysis carried out by the Crown Prosecution Service in England and Wales in 2020 found that most stalking offences are committed by abusive ex-partners. It was found that 84 per cent of stalking cases sampled at random from across England and Wales involved complaints against ex-partners and in 75 per cent of cases, domestic abuse had previously been reported during the relationship.[83] In England and Wales, the Protection from Harassment Act 1997 was amended by the Protection of Freedoms Act 2012 to include an offence of stalking under section 2A and also an offence of stalking involving fear of violence or serious alarm or distress under section 4A. In Scotland, an offence of stalking is contained in section 39 of the Criminal Justice and Licensing (Scotland) Act 2010. However, until the passing of the Protection from Stalking Act (Northern Ireland) 2022 (as will be discussed in Chapter 4) there was no specific offence of stalking in Northern Ireland. Instead, the more general offences of harassment as found in article 4 of the Protection from Harassment (Northern Ireland) Order 1997 and putting people in fear of violence as found in article 6 of the Order, had to be relied upon in cases involving stalking.

In 2016 the then Justice Minister, Claire Sugden MLA, commissioned a review of the law relating to stalking in Northern Ireland, and in September of that year the Northern Ireland Assembly debated a motion on stalking. The Committee for Justice then initiated its own review of the law to determine whether specific stalking offences should be enacted. Although the Committee was due to conclude its review in April 2017 and subsequently publish its findings, the suspension of the Assembly from January 2017 meant that this review was not completed. However, the Department of Justice's review team built on the work of the Justice Committee and proceeded to review the existing legislative framework; engage with other jurisdictions regarding their approaches to stalking; and develop proposals. A Stalking Reference Group of key stakeholders was set up, and contributed to the review by considering types of stalking behaviours and their impact on victims; highlighting the experiences of victims under the current law; identifying aspects of the law that potentially needed to be changed; and ensuring that a wide range of policy options were considered. In November 2018, the Department of Justice launched a public consultation on the creation of a new offence of stalking in Northern Ireland. A report of the consultation and a summary of responses was published in November 2019.[84] 93 per cent of respondents to the consultation were of the view that the current legislative position was insufficient.[85] The Department thus concluded that it would be recommending to an incoming Justice Minister that a stalking bill containing provisions to give effect to the introduction of a new specific offence of stalking and to stalking protection orders, be developed for introduction to a future Assembly. The Department stated that it would also 'continue to raise the profile of stalking by sharing best practice models and guidance, in use in other jurisdictions, with operational partners'.[86]

Domestic Homicide Reviews

Although the majority of the Domestic Violence, Crime and Victims Act 2004 applies only to England and Wales, certain provisions of this legislation apply also to Northern Ireland, among them being section 9 which makes provision for the introduction of domestic homicide reviews. Under section 9, a domestic homicide review is a review of the circumstances in which the death of a person aged 16 or over has, or appears to have, resulted from violence, abuse or neglect by a person to whom they were related; a person with whom they were, or had been, in an intimate personal relationship; or a member of the same household. The purpose of a domestic homicide review is to identify lessons which can be learnt from the death. Domestic homicide reviews were subsequently introduced in England and Wales in 2011.[87]

In July 2018, the Department of Justice launched a consultation seeking views on a proposed model for the introduction of domestic homicide reviews in Northern Ireland.[88] A summary of responses to the consultation was published in January 2019.[89] Those who responded to the consultation were unanimously in support of the introduction of domestic homicide reviews to Northern Ireland. Respondents recognised that the purpose of such reviews was not to apportion blame or to investigate the conduct of individuals, but instead that it was to understand the context and environment in which the relevant professionals made decisions, and took or did not take action. Respondents were also in agreement that the overarching purpose of domestic homicide reviews was to prevent the occurrence of future domestic homicides and to improve service responses for all victims of domestic abuse and their children.[90]

It was established that the Department of Justice would proceed to work with the Domestic Homicide Review Task and Finish Group to finalise a domestic homicide review model which was reflective of respondents' comments; finalise a governance arrangements document and also multi-agency guidance; consider whether additional training for those inputting into the review was necessary, or if the guidance would be sufficient; develop a job specification for the Chairperson for the reviews and begin a recruitment exercise for this position; and commence the relevant provision under the Domestic Violence, Crimes and Victims Act 2004.[91]

Criminal Justice Inspection Northern Ireland Report – June 2019

In June 2019, CJINI published another report on the handling of domestic violence and abuse cases by the criminal justice system in Northern Ireland.[92] The report noted that the Departments of Justice and Health had published 'Stopping Domestic and Sexual Violence and Abuse in Northern Ireland: A Seven Year Strategy' in March 2016. In 2015 the creation of C7 Public Protection Branch by the PSNI had brought together officers in public protection roles, and the new role of Domestic Abuse and Adult Safeguarding (DAAS) officer had been created. The work of domestic abuse policing had been deemed to be a specialist detective role and officers had undergone the appropriate development programme. All officers received training on domestic offences through the Foundation Training programme. The PSNI was an active partner in the MARAC process, both chairing the meetings and providing coordination and administrative support. There was evidence that PSNI investigations were carried out in a timely manner in the large majority of cases, and body-worn video had been rolled out and had provided valuable evidence. There was also evidence of governance and management oversight in district policing as regards domestic abuse cases. Police took a victim statement in a timely manner in the majority of cases, and the submission of the prosecution file to the PPS was in accordance with the PSNI's time limits in 80 per cent of cases. Generally, most domestic abuse cases progressed effectively. Victims highlighted the support received from organisations such as Women's Aid and Victim Support as being essential to them both before and during the criminal justice process, and positive relationships had been developed between the PSNI and victim supporters. The latter advised that the police response had improved since the previous inspection by CJINI.[93]

However, seven recommendations were made in relation to improvements which were still deemed by CJINI to be necessary. According to CJINI, the PSNI should develop an action plan within six months, to develop further the approach to dealing with cases of domestic abuse and address issues highlighted as regards the training and development of new recruits and first responders in relation to coercive and controlling behaviour, harassment and stalking behaviour; and risk assessment practices in cases of domestic abuse. In addition, CJINI recommended that the PSNI and the MARAC Operational Board should also develop an action plan within six months, to develop further the multi-agency safeguarding arrangements for cases of domestic abuse in Northern Ireland. It was recommended that the PSNI and the PPS should within three months, develop an implementation plan to develop further the prosecution team approach for cases involving domestic abuse or with a domestic motivation. In addition, the Criminal Justice Board, in conjunction with its partners, should, in the nine months following the report, ensure the delivery and roll out of Northern Ireland-wide schemes to enable the clustering of domestic abuse cases to a designated court in each Administrative Court Division; and a properly costed contract for an Independent Domestic Violence Advisor service to address the safety of victims at high risk of harm. Also, the Department of Justice should review how potential inadequacies in current legislation regarding the act of choking or strangulation could be addressed; and develop plans for legislation to introduce protection orders for stalking and harassment. In addition, the PPS should review the use of special measures in cases of domestic abuse and take action to address any issues arising.[94]

Conclusion

In conclusion, by the end of 2019 the response of the criminal justice system in Northern Ireland to domestic abuse had certainly developed greatly. During the dark days of the 'Troubles', this issue had received very little attention from the criminal justice system, with resources being focused instead on addressing the political violence which engulfed Northern Ireland for around 30 years. However, the signing of the Good Friday Agreement in 1998, and the subsequent establishment of the devolved Assembly, opened the way for other matters to receive attention, including the abuse which many people were suffering within their own homes. Initiatives such as the DVADS were certainly important steps in this process.

It is notable that in a comparison of studies carried out in 1992[95] and 2016 involving interviews with victims of domestic abuse, Doyle and McWilliams found that the majority of participants in the 2016 study reported that their experiences with the police had been positive, with 62.5 per cent of participants who had contacted the police describing them as 'helpful', 30 per cent of participants describing them as 'not helpful' and the remaining 7.5 per cent reporting 'mixed' experiences. By contrast, in the 1992 study, only 25.7 per cent of participants described the police as being 'helpful', with the remaining 74.3 per cent of participants describing them as 'not helpful'.[96] Also, in the 2016 study, most participants who had contacted the police said that official action had been taken, such as arresting the perpetrator (in 35 per cent of cases) or issuing them with an official caution (in 32.5 per cent of cases). In the 1992 study, by contrast, few participants reported that the police took official action, with only 8.6 per cent of respondents reporting that the police had arrested the perpetrator and another 8.6 per cent reporting that the police had issued an official caution.[97]

Nevertheless, difficulties remained, particularly in relation to the lack of legislation criminalising coercive control. It is noteworthy that in the 2016 study discussed by Doyle and McWilliams, several participants reported that while the police responded in a helpful manner when an incident involved physical violence, 'they were often quite dismissive' when an incident involved psychological abuse.[98]

However, as a new decade dawned, it was impossible to predict that in just a few short months, the whole world would change. Chapter 4 will provide a detailed discussion of the impact of the events of 2020–2022 on victims of domestic abuse in Northern Ireland, and will analyse the response of the criminal justice system to domestic abuse during this period.

Notes

1 Criminal Justice Inspection Northern Ireland, 'Domestic Violence and Abuse', December 2010, www.cjini.org/getattachment/1b651b43-657b-471b-b320-101fca7c6930/Domestic-Violence-and-Abuse.aspx; Criminal Justice Inspection Northern Ireland, 'Domestic Violence and Abuse – A Follow Up Review', October 2013, www.cjini.org/getattachment/34118bcc-00c5-4071-bf2f-5397e6b20332/report.aspx; Criminal Justice Inspection Northern Ireland, 'No Excuse', June 2019, www.cjini.org/getattachment/079beabb-d094-40e9-8738-0f84cd347ae8/report.aspx

2 Department of Justice, 'Domestic Abuse Offence and Domestic Violence Disclosure Scheme – A Consultation', 5 February 2016, www.justice-ni.gov.uk/sites/default/files/consultations/doj/consultation-domestic-violence.PDF
3 Department of Justice, 'Stalking – A Serious Concern. A Consultation on the Creation of a New Offence of Stalking in Northern Ireland. Consultation Report and Summary of Responses', 1 November 2019, www.justice-ni.gov.uk/sites/default/files/publications/justice/stalking-consultation-report-responses.pdf
4 Burton M., *Legal Responses to Domestic Violence*, 2008, Routledge, Abingdon, at 2.
5 McWilliams M. and Ní Aoláin F., '"There is a war going on you know": Addressing the complexity of violence against women in conflicted and post conflict societies', (2013) 1 *Transitional Justice Review* 4 at 27. For further discussion of domestic abuse in Northern Ireland during this time, see McWilliams M. and McKiernan J., *Bringing It Out in the Open: Domestic Violence in Northern Ireland*, 1993, HMSO, Belfast; and Evason E., *Hidden Violence: A Study of Battered Women in Northern Ireland*, 1982, Farset Co-op Press, Belfast.
6 The Agreement can be accessed at assets.publishing.service.gov.uk/government/uploads/system/uploads/attachment_data/file/136652/agreement.pdf
7 Good Friday Agreement, 'Policing and Justice' section, para. 5.
8 Criminal Justice Inspection Northern Ireland, www.cjini.org/.
9 Criminal Justice Inspection Northern Ireland (2010), op. cit.
10 Department of Health and Social Services and Northern Ireland Office, 'Tackling Domestic Violence – A Policy for Northern Ireland', 1995.
11 Criminal Justice Inspection Northern Ireland (2010), op. cit., at vii.
12 Criminal Justice Inspection Northern Ireland (2010), op. cit., at vii–viii.
13 Criminal Justice Inspection Northern Ireland (2010), op. cit., at viii.
14 Criminal Justice Inspection Northern Ireland (2010), op. cit., at viii.
15 Criminal Justice Inspection Northern Ireland (2010), op. cit., at ix.
16 Criminal Justice Inspection Northern Ireland (2010), op. cit., at para. 2.21.
17 Criminal Justice Inspection Northern Ireland (2010), op. cit., at para. 2.26.
18 Criminal Justice Inspection Northern Ireland (2010), op. cit., at para. 3.4.
19 Criminal Justice Inspection Northern Ireland (2010), op. cit., at para. 4.8.
20 Criminal Justice Inspection Northern Ireland (2010), op. cit., at para. 4.12.
21 Criminal Justice Inspection Northern Ireland (2010), op. cit., at para. 5.4.
22 Criminal Justice Inspection Northern Ireland (2010), op. cit., at para. 5.12.
23 Criminal Justice Inspection Northern Ireland (2010), op. cit., at para. 6.2.
24 Criminal Justice Inspection Northern Ireland (2010), op. cit., at para. 2.11.
25 Criminal Justice Inspection Northern Ireland (2010), op. cit., at para. 2.17.
26 Criminal Justice Inspection Northern Ireland (2010), op. cit., at para. 2.18.
27 Criminal Justice Inspection Northern Ireland (2010), op. cit., at para. 3.13.
28 Criminal Justice Inspection Northern Ireland (2010), op. cit., at para. 5.8.
29 Criminal Justice Inspection Northern Ireland (2013), op. cit.
30 Criminal Justice Inspection Northern Ireland (2013), op. cit., at 10–11.
31 Criminal Justice Inspection Northern Ireland (2013), op. cit., at 8.

32 Criminal Justice Inspection Northern Ireland (2013), op. cit., at 9.
33 Criminal Justice Inspection Northern Ireland (2013), op. cit., at 11–12.
34 Criminal Justice Inspection Northern Ireland (2013), op. cit., at 12–13.
35 Criminal Justice Inspection Northern Ireland (2013), op. cit., at 13–14.
36 Criminal Justice Inspection Northern Ireland (2013), op. cit., at 17.
37 Criminal Justice Inspection Northern Ireland (2013), op. cit., at 17–18.
38 Criminal Justice Inspection Northern Ireland (2013), op. cit., at 9.
39 Criminal Justice Inspection Northern Ireland (2013), op. cit., at 10.
40 Criminal Justice Inspection Northern Ireland (2013), op. cit., at 14–15.
41 Criminal Justice Inspection Northern Ireland (2013), op. cit., at 15.
42 Criminal Justice Inspection Northern Ireland (2013), op. cit., at 16.
43 Criminal Justice Inspection Northern Ireland (2013), op. cit., at 16–17.
44 Criminal Justice Inspection Northern Ireland (2013), op. cit., at 4.
45 Criminal Justice Inspection Northern Ireland (2013), op. cit., at 19.
46 Criminal Justice Inspection Northern Ireland (2013), op. cit., at 19.
47 Criminal Justice Inspection Northern Ireland (2013), op. cit., at 19.
48 Department of Health, Social Services and Public Safety and Department of Justice, 'Stopping Domestic and Sexual Violence and Abuse in Northern Ireland – A Seven Year Strategy', March 2016, www.justice-ni.gov.uk/sites/default/files/publications/doj/stopping-domestic-sexual-violence-ni.pdf
49 Department of Health, Social Services and Public Safety and Department of Justice, op. cit., at 63.
50 [1997] 4 All ER 225.
51 Burton op. cit., at 61.
52 (2006) 2 Cr App R 24.
53 See Burton, op. cit., at 62. For further discussion of the concept of 'bodily harm', see Bishop C., 'Domestic Violence: The Limitations of a Legal Response', in S. Hilder and V. Bettinson (eds.), *Domestic Violence – Interdisciplinary Perspectives on Protection, Prevention and Intervention*, 2016, Palgrave Macmillan, London, 59–79 at 70–71.
54 For discussion of the concept of coercive control, see Stark E., *Coercive Control: How Men Trap Women in Personal Life*, 2007, Oxford University Press, Oxford; Stark E., 'Rethinking coercive control', (2009) 15 *Violence Against Women* 1509; Williamson E., 'Living in the world of the domestic violence perpetrator: Negotiating the unreality of coercive control', (2010) 16 *Violence Against Women* 1412; Stark E., 'Looking beyond domestic violence: Policing coercive control', (2012) 12 *Journal of Police Crisis Negotiations* 199; and Stark E. and Hester M., 'Coercive control: Update and review', (2019) 25 *Violence Against Women* 81.
55 See for example, Tadros V., 'The Distinctiveness of Domestic Abuse: A Freedom Based Account' in A. Duff and S. Green (eds.), *Defining Crimes*, 2005, Oxford University Press, Oxford, 119–142; Tolmie J.R., 'Coercive Control: To Criminalize or not to Criminalize?', (2018) 18 *Criminology and Criminal Justice* 50; and Bettinson V. and Bishop C., 'Is the creation of a discrete offence of coercive control necessary to combat domestic violence?', (2015) 66 *Northern Ireland Legal Quarterly* 179.

56 For discussion of section 76 of the Serious Crime Act 2015, see Bettinson V. and Robson J., 'Prosecuting coercive control: Reforming storytelling in the courtroom', (2020) 12 *Criminal Law Review* 1107; McGorrery P. and McMahon M., 'Criminalising "the worst" part: Operationalising the offence of coercive control in England and Wales', (2019) 11 *Criminal Law Review* 957; Bettinson V., 'Aligning partial defences to murder with the offence of coercive or controlling behaviour', (2019) 83 *Journal of Criminal Law* 71; and Bishop C. and Bettinson V., 'Evidencing domestic violence, including behaviour that falls under the new offence of "coercive and controlling behaviour"', (2018) 22 *International Journal of Evidence and Proof* 3.

57 For discussion of the Domestic Abuse (Scotland) Act 2018, see Cairns I., 'The *Moorov* doctrine and coercive control: Proving a "course of behaviour" under s.1 of the Domestic Abuse (Scotland) Act 2018', (2020) 24 *International Journal of Evidence and Proof* 396; Forbes E.E., 'The Domestic Abuse (Scotland) Act 2018: The whole story?', (2018) 22 *Edinburgh Law Review* 406; Cairns I., 'What counts as "domestic"? Family relationships and the proposed criminalization of domestic abuse in Scotland', (2017) 21 *Edinburgh Law Review* 262; and Hughes M., 'The Domestic Abuse (Scotland) Act 2018: A general guide and civil ramifications', (2019) 20 *Scots Law Times* 59.

58 Application no. 41261/17, judgment of 9 July 2019, para. 75.

59 Article 3 states that, 'No one shall be subjected to torture or to inhuman or degrading treatment or punishment'.

60 Committee on the Elimination of Discrimination Against Women, General Recommendation No. 19: Violence Against Women (1992), para. 6.

61 Committee on the Elimination of Discrimination Against Women, 'Concluding observations on the eighth periodic report of the United Kingdom of Great Britain and Northern Ireland', CEDAW/C/GBR/CO/8 (14 March 2019) para. 30(b).

62 Department of Justice (2016), op. cit.

63 Department of Justice, 'Domestic Abuse Offence and Domestic Violence Disclosure Scheme – A Consultation, Summary of Responses', 2016, www.justice-ni.gov.uk/sites/default/files/consultations/justice/domestic-abuse-offence-domestic-violence-disclosure-scheme-summary-of-responses.pdf, para. 1.9.

64 Department of Justice, 'Domestic Abuse Offence and Domestic Violence Disclosure Scheme – A Consultation, Summary of Responses', 2016, op. cit., at para. 1.10.

65 Department of Justice, 'Domestic Abuse Offence and Domestic Violence Disclosure Scheme – A Consultation, Summary of Responses', 2016, op. cit., at para. 1.11.

66 Department of Justice, 'Domestic Abuse Offence and Domestic Violence Disclosure Scheme – A Consultation, Summary of Responses', 2016, op. cit., at para. 1.12.

67 Department of Justice, 'Domestic Abuse Offence and Domestic Violence Disclosure Scheme – A Consultation, Summary of Responses', 2016, op. cit., at para. 1.13.
68 Department of Justice, 'Domestic Abuse Offence and Domestic Violence Disclosure Scheme – A Consultation, Summary of Responses', 2016, op. cit., at para. 1.14.
69 See BBC News, 'New Abuse Law 'Held Up by Lack of NI Assembly', 19 January 2018, www.bbc.co.uk/news/uk-northern-ireland-42739589
70 For discussion of the domestic violence disclosure scheme in England and Wales, see Grace J., 'Clare's Law, or the national Domestic Violence Disclosure Scheme: The contested legalities of criminality information sharing', (2015) 79 *Journal of Criminal Law* 36; and Duggan M. and Grace J., 'Assessing vulnerabilities in the Domestic Violence Disclosure Scheme', (2018) 30 *Child and Family Law Quarterly* 145.
71 Department of Justice, 'Domestic Abuse Offence and Domestic Violence Disclosure Scheme – A Consultation, Summary of Responses', 2016, op. cit., at para. 1.19.
72 Department of Justice, 'Domestic Abuse Offence and Domestic Violence Disclosure Scheme – A Consultation, Summary of Responses', 2016, op. cit., at para. 1.20.
73 Department of Justice, 'Domestic Abuse Offence and Domestic Violence Disclosure Scheme – A Consultation, Summary of Responses', 2016, op. cit., at para. 1.21.
74 Department of Justice, 'Domestic Abuse Offence and Domestic Violence Disclosure Scheme – A Consultation, Summary of Responses', 2016, op. cit., at para. 1.22.
75 Department of Justice, 'Domestic Abuse Offence and Domestic Violence Disclosure Scheme – A Consultation, Summary of Responses', 2016, op. cit., at para. 1.23.
76 Department of Justice, 'Domestic Abuse Offence and Domestic Violence Disclosure Scheme – A Consultation, Summary of Responses', 2016, op. cit., at para. 1.25.
77 Department of Justice, 'Domestic Abuse Offence and Domestic Violence Disclosure Scheme – A Consultation, Summary of Responses', 2016, op. cit., at para. 1.26.
78 Department of Justice, 'Domestic Abuse Offence and Domestic Violence Disclosure Scheme – A Consultation, Summary of Responses', 2016, op. cit., at para. 1.27.
79 Department of Justice, 'Domestic Violence and Abuse Disclosure Scheme Northern Ireland (DVADS NI) Guidance', March 2018, www.justice-ni.gov.uk/sites/default/files/publications/justice/Domestic-violence-and-abuse-disclose-scheme.pdf, para. 4.6.
80 Department of Justice (2018), op. cit., at para. 4.7.
81 Department of Justice (2018), op. cit., at para. 4.7.
82 Northern Ireland Executive, '326 Checks Carried Out in the Last Year through the Domestic Violence and Abuse Disclosure Scheme', 26 March

2019, www.northernireland.gov.uk/news/326-checks-carried-out-last-year-through-domestic-violence-and-abuse-disclosure-scheme

83 Crown Prosecution Service, 'Stalking Analysis Reveals Domestic Abuse Link', 4 December 2020, www.cps.gov.uk/cps/news/stalking-analysis-reveals-domestic-abuse-link. See also Humphreys C. and Thiara R.K., 'Neither justice nor protection: Women's experiences of post-separation violence', (2003) 25 *Journal of Social Welfare and Family Law* 195.

84 Department of Justice, 'Stalking – A Serious Concern. A Consultation on the Creation of a New Offence of Stalking in Northern Ireland. Consultation Report and Summary of Responses', 1 November 2019, www.justice-ni.gov.uk/sites/default/files/publications/justice/stalking-consultation-report-responses.pdf, 3–4.

85 Department of Justice (2019), op. cit., at 5.

86 Department of Justice (2019), op. cit., at 21.

87 For further information on domestic homicide reviews in England and Wales, see www.gov.uk/government/collections/domestic-homicide-review

88 Department of Justice, 'Domestic Homicide Reviews – Consultation', July 2018, www.justice-ni.gov.uk/sites/default/files/consultations/justice/dhr-consultation.pdf

89 Department of Justice, 'Domestic Homicide Reviews – A Consultation. Summary of Responses and Way Forward', January 2019, www.justice-ni.gov.uk/sites/default/files/consultations/justice/dhr-summary-of-responses.pdf

90 Department of Justice, 'Domestic Homicide Reviews – A Consultation. Summary of Responses and Way Forward', 2019, op. cit., at para. 1.10.

91 Department of Justice, 'Domestic Homicide Reviews – A Consultation. Summary of Responses and Way Forward', 2019, op. cit., at para. 1.21.

92 Criminal Justice Inspection Northern Ireland (2019), op. cit.

93 Criminal Justice Inspection Northern Ireland (2019), op. cit., at 7–11.

94 Criminal Justice Inspection Northern Ireland (2019), op. cit., at 12–13.

95 McWilliams and McKiernan, op. cit.

96 Doyle J.L. and McWilliams M., 'What difference does peace make? Intimate partner violence and violent conflict in Northern Ireland', (2020) 26 *Violence Against Women* 139 at 148.

97 Doyle and McWilliams, op. cit., at 149–150.

98 Doyle and McWilliams, op. cit., at 151.

4 Criminal Justice Responses to Domestic Abuse in Northern Ireland 2020–2022

This chapter seeks to analyse the responses of the criminal justice system in Northern Ireland to domestic abuse from the beginning of 2020 until the elections to the Northern Ireland Assembly on 5 May 2022. The Assembly was restored in January 2020 following a hiatus of three years, and from March 2020 levels of domestic abuse in Northern Ireland began to rise significantly, in the context of the lockdown measures which were adopted as a response to the COVID-19 pandemic. The chapter discusses these increased levels of domestic abuse and analyses the ways in which the criminal justice system responded.

A number of very positive steps were taken during 2020–2022 as regards responses to domestic abuse in Northern Ireland, such as the introduction of domestic homicide reviews. In addition, a specific offence of domestic abuse was introduced in March 2021 under section 1 of the Domestic Abuse and Civil Proceedings Act (Northern Ireland) 2021. The new legislation has the effect of criminalising coercive and controlling behaviour, thus bringing Northern Ireland into line with the other jurisdictions within the UK and Ireland in this regard, and also with relevant human rights standards as regards legislative responses to domestic abuse, as were set out in Chapter 2. The implications of the 2021 Act for Northern Ireland's response to domestic abuse will be discussed in detail. However, although the enactment of the domestic abuse offence is certainly a very positive development, this will not constitute a panacea to the problem of domestic abuse in Northern Ireland. Legislation in itself is insufficient in relation to addressing this issue, and further sustained efforts are necessary to improve the responses of the criminal justice system in Northern Ireland to domestic abuse.

DOI: 10.4324/9781003261650-4

Northern Ireland in Early 2020 – The Onset of COVID-19

The Northern Ireland Assembly, which had collapsed in January 2017, was restored in January 2020 following the signing of the 'New Decade, New Approach' agreement.[1] The outlook for Northern Ireland seemed bright. Some news reports had trickled in of a strange new illness called 'Coronavirus', but these cases were far away, on the other side of the world.

However, this new virus seemed to be spreading and appeared to be impossible to contain. On 27 February 2020 the first case of Coronavirus was identified in Northern Ireland. This deadly virus had somehow travelled from the far side of the world to this jurisdiction. The importance of hand hygiene was emphasised; hand sanitiser became like 'gold dust'; and shoppers began stocking up on food, paracetamol and other essential items…just in case. Then, suddenly, the world changed. Prime Minister Boris Johnson's instruction of 23 March 2020 was stark – 'You must stay at home'. Lockdown restrictions were announced for Northern Ireland, along with the rest of the UK. According to government guidance, people should only leave home for very limited reasons – shopping for basic necessities such as food and medicine; one form of exercise per day; medical need, or to provide care or help to a vulnerable person; and travelling to and from work, but only when work could not be done from home. Even when the activity in question fell within one of these four categories, the amount of time spent away from home had to be minimised as far as possible.[2] Such lockdown measures were indisputably essential. At the time when these restrictions were implemented, 335 people in the UK had died as a result of contracting Coronavirus.[3] This was a deadly virus about which little was known, and for which there were no vaccines and no effective treatments. In such circumstances, lockdown measures were the only option available. In order to reduce the spread of the virus, the best course of action was to keep people apart as much as possible. In the absence of interaction, a virus cannot spread.

And so the war began – a war fought not in a foreign land against a visible enemy with guns and tanks; but a war fought in hospitals, care homes and private residences against an invisible virus. The oft-repeated mantra was, 'Stay at home; protect the National Health Service (NHS); save lives', and this was exactly what the large majority of people did. Things which had previously been taken for granted – visiting family members, attending church services, going to the hairdresser – suddenly became impermissible, and a situation which many had thought would last only a few weeks stretched to months, and then to a year and beyond. New terms such as 'self-isolation', 'social distancing' and 'track and trace' became embedded into the language; and in common parlance 'Coronavirus' became 'COVID-19' and then simply 'COVID'. Lockdown measures eased at various intervals, although to many this made little difference – the virus remained a threat.

However, there was hope. Scientists were working on vaccines and in January 2021 the first doses began to be administered to people in Northern Ireland. By the end of 2021, in Northern Ireland there had been 394,854 confirmed cases and 2,979 deaths due to the virus.[4] The war against COVID-19 is not yet over, but vaccines are a powerful weapon in the fight.

The Impact of the COVID-19 Pandemic on Levels of Domestic Abuse in Northern Ireland

However, the full impact of the COVID-19 pandemic on the health of the people of Northern Ireland extends far beyond cases of the virus itself. Domestic abuse is well-recognised as constituting a health issue, and in April 2020, the World Health Organization stated that 'violence against women remains a major threat to global public health and women's health during emergencies'.[5] Gender-based violence, including domestic abuse, has been recognised as being a health issue by the international human rights bodies. Article 12(1) of the International Covenant on Economic, Social and Cultural Rights (ICESCR) contains the right 'to the enjoyment of the highest attainable standard of physical and mental health'. In 2000 the Committee on Economic, Social and Cultural Rights (CESCR), the monitoring body of the ICESCR, issued General Comment No. 14 in which it elaborated upon its interpretation of Article 12. In this document, the Committee stated that,

> To eliminate discrimination against women, there is a need to develop and implement a comprehensive national strategy for promoting women's right to health throughout their life span...A major health goal should be reducing women's health risks, particularly lowering rates of maternal mortality and protecting women from domestic violence.[6]

The Committee proceeded explicitly to link gender-based violence and the right to health, asserting that a failure to protect women against violence or to prosecute perpetrators would constitute a violation of the duty to protect the right to health.[7]

In addition, Article 12(1) of CEDAW places an obligation on States Parties to 'take all appropriate measures to eliminate discrimination against women in the field of health care in order to ensure, on a basis of equality of men and women, access to health care services'. In 1999 the CEDAW Committee issued its General Recommendation No. 24, the purpose of which was to set out the Committee's views on the obligations entailed by Article 12. In General Recommendation No. 24, the Committee stated that Article 12 implies an obligation to respect, protect and fulfil women's rights to health care,[8] and that the duty to protect rights relating to women's health requires States Parties to take action to prevent and impose sanctions for breaches of rights by private persons and organisations.[9] The Committee then proceeded explicitly to link the area of health to gender-based violence, asserting that:

> Since gender-based violence is a critical health issue for women, States parties should ensure:
>
> (a) The enactment and effective enforcement of laws and the formulation of policies, including health care protocols and hospital procedures to address violence against women and abuse of girl children and the provision of appropriate health services;
> (b) Gender-sensitive training to enable health care workers to detect and manage the health consequences of gender-based violence.[10]

The international bodies have also called upon governments to collaborate with health services as regards the issue of gender-based violence, including domestic abuse. For example, in 1990 the UN General Assembly urged States 'to begin or continue to explore, develop and implement multidisciplinary policies, measures and strategies… with respect to domestic violence in all its facets, including…health-related…aspects'.[11]

It was immediately apparent to those working in the area of combating domestic abuse that lockdown measures could be disastrous for victims. Measures mandating that people should only leave their homes when it was essential to do so, would result in circumstances in which many victims of domestic abuse would be further isolated with their abusers. Whilst previously either the victim or the abuser, or both, may have gone out to work, the move to working from home where possible would have the impact of closing off even this method of escape. Indeed, even the very act of contacting support services would be made more difficult, due to fears of being overheard. Also, the fact that people could not mix with those from another household would cut off important sources of support for victims of abuse. A common tactic of perpetrators of domestic abuse is to isolate victims from their support networks. For example, in research carried out by Doyle and McWilliams in 2016, it was found that 86 per cent of victims of domestic abuse surveyed reported that their partner had prevented them from contacting or seeing their friends and families.[12] The lockdown measures would do this without the necessity for any action whatsoever on the part of abusers.

On 20 March 2020, at a time when 'stay at home' messages were still in the form of government advice only, Women's Aid Federation Northern Ireland issued a statement which asserted that:

> We know that the government's advice on self or household-isolation will have a direct impact on women and children experiencing domestic violence and abuse in Northern Ireland. Home is often not a safe place for survivors of domestic violence and abuse. We are concerned that social distancing and self-isolation will be used as a tool of coercive and controlling behaviour by perpetrators and will shut down routes to safety and support.[13]

In addition, the statement remarked that, 'The impact of self-isolation will also have a direct impact on specialist services, who are already operating in an extremely challenging funding climate and will be rightly concerned about how to continue delivering life-saving support during the pandemic'.

Women's Aid thus called for workers within frontline domestic abuse services to be recognised as 'key workers', and for safety advice and planning for those experiencing domestic abuse to be included in national government advice on COVID-19. Women's Aid also called upon the Northern Ireland Assembly to consider the safety and needs of victims of domestic abuse and relevant services as a fundamental priority within guidance and contingency planning for the pandemic, and welcomed an announcement from the Department of Communities, which funds refugees and outreach services, that there would be no impact to the community and voluntary sector.

It soon became apparent that the predictions made by Women's Aid were correct. Since the onset of the COVID-19 pandemic, incidents of domestic abuse have increased significantly in Northern Ireland. According to statistics released by the PSNI, there were 31,848 domestic abuse incidents in Northern Ireland during 2020, one of the highest rates since such records began in 2004/05.[14] Since the first lockdown in this jurisdiction began on 23 March 2020, the PSNI had by May of that year received at least 3,755 calls in relation to domestic abuse.[15] From 1 April until 21 April 2020, the PSNI received 1,919 calls regarding domestic abuse, which represented an increase of 10 per cent on the approximate number of 570 calls which were normally received each week prior to the onset of the COVID-19 pandemic. By the end of April 2020, three people had been killed as a result of domestic abuse since the beginning of the first lockdown.[16] On 23 March 2021, Women's Aid Federation Northern Ireland joined with a number of other organisations working in the area of combating domestic abuse to issue a statement asserting that:

> It was clear from the outset that lockdown measures would exacerbate women and girls' experiences of violence and abuse, and shut down routes to safety and support. Over the past year this has been borne out in the huge increases in demand our sector has witnessed, the increasing complexity of need from those we support, the strains that frontline workers have faced in responding to survivors in trauma, the new ways that perpetrators are using Covid-19 as tools for abuse and control, and of course the tragic murders of women and children that we remember today.[17]

It is of course crucial to bear in mind that domestic abuse is caused by the actions of perpetrators, and the COVID-19 pandemic and the resulting lockdown measures must never be viewed as in any way whatsoever negating the responsibility of abusers for their actions. Nevertheless, it is true that the lockdown measures in Northern Ireland, as in many other States around the globe, provided circumstances which exacerbated the suffering of many victims of domestic abuse.

Responses to the Rise in Levels of Domestic Abuse in Northern Ireland in the Context of the COVID-19 Pandemic

As was discussed in Chapter 2, various statements have been issued by UN and regional human rights bodies in response to the increased levels of domestic abuse during the COVID-19 pandemic. For example, in March 2020, the UN Special Rapporteur on violence against women, its causes and consequences, issued a statement on domestic abuse in the context of COVID-19 lockdowns,[18] in which she called upon governments not to put the protection of victims on hold and urged them to continue to combat domestic abuse in the time of

COVID-19. In April 2020, the CEDAW Committee issued a guidance note on CEDAW and COVID-19, in which it stressed that even during the pandemic, States Parties still had 'a due diligence obligation to prevent and protect women from, and hold perpetrators accountable for, gender-based violence against women'.[19] States should therefore ensure that victims of gender-based violence still had effective access to justice.

Measures were certainly adopted by the government in Northern Ireland to address the issue of domestic abuse since the onset of the COVID-19 pandemic. For example, although the work of the courts had been severely affected by the pandemic, emergency applications for non-molestation orders and restraining orders could still be made through the Family Proceedings courts. Steps were taken by both the Northern Ireland Department of Justice and the PSNI to raise awareness among victims of domestic abuse that help and support was still available.[20] For instance, the Departments of Justice and Health issued guidance stating that household isolation instructions introduced as a result of the COVID-19 pandemic did not apply if a person needed to leave their home to escape from domestic abuse.[21] This guidance also provided advice on what domestic abuse is; what signs to look for; and where help and support could be obtained.

The Department of Justice implemented a media campaign entitled 'See the Signs', whilst the PSNI continued with their media campaign termed 'Behind Closed Doors'. The PSNI created an animated video for this campaign which explained how domestic abuse can take many forms and which was circulated widely during the lockdown period, and maintained a strong online presence with the aim of providing continuous reassurance to victims that help remained available.[22]

The PSNI also continued collaborative working with key stakeholders such as Women's Aid and the Men's Advisory Project to spread awareness of crucial information for victims, such as in relation to the 24-hour Domestic and Sexual Abuse Helpline.[23] The PSNI led a multi-agency proactive operational response, in collaboration with the Departments of Justice, Health and Communities as well as voluntary sector partners, with the aim of ensuring a joined-up approach to the prevention of harm and the provision of support.[24] For example, the PSNI, in collaboration with Women's Aid and in conjunction with the Northern Ireland Housing Executive, established 'crash pads' in Belfast, Ballymena and Lisburn to enable a safe environment of self-isolation for victims of domestic abuse suffering with COVID-19.[25] Also, the PSNI met weekly with the Domestic Abuse Independent Advisory Group, the members of which included the Public Prosecution

Service (PPS), the Northern Ireland Courts and Tribunals Service and organisations such as Women's Aid and the Men's Advisory Project, in order to discuss the levels of demand and pressure on the PSNI and other relevant bodies.[26]

In terms of support for victims, prior to the COVID-19 pandemic, the PSNI under its 'victim call back' system would 'call back' victims within approximately ten days. However, the PSNI revised this during the lockdown period and reduced the average time taken to call victims to within 24 hours.[27] The PSNI also continued the 'Safe Place' initiative, which provides support for those needing information on domestic abuse. All PSNI stations are designated as 'Safe Places' and as a 'Safe Place' organisation the PSNI is committed to supporting the 'Safe Place' campaign pledge never to commit, condone or stay silent about domestic abuse; to providing a safe place for victims of domestic abuse to access information confidentially; to acknowledging that domestic abuse is an issue that impacts on society as a whole; and to being prepared to play a part in supporting victims and stating clearly to perpetrators that abuse will not be tolerated.[28]

The measures adopted by the PSNI to further collaborative working with other bodies and agencies are certainly meritorious and very much to be welcomed. As the Northern Ireland Policing Board commented in its 'Report on the Thematic Review of the Policing Response to COVID-19', 'The PSNI should ensure that the innovation, progress and learning made in developing new approaches to collaborative working for vulnerable people during the pandemic emergency period is harnessed and used to inform better collaboration in the future'.[29]

It is also of note that the 'Ask for ANI' scheme, a UK-wide initiative which was launched on 14 January 2021, enables victims of domestic abuse to use the code word 'ANI' ('Action Needed Immediately') in participating pharmacies to let staff know that they need to access support. When the code word is used, a trained member of staff offers a private space for the victim to phone either the police or support services such as a domestic abuse helpline. The staff member also offers to assist the victim in doing so. When launching the scheme, the Prime Minister, Boris Johnson, commented that:

> As we once again have to ask people across the country to stay at home to tackle this virus, it's vital that we take action to protect those for who home is not a safe space. That is why we have launched this scheme, supported by pharmacies up and down the

> country, to give some of the most vulnerable people in society a critical lifeline – making sure they have access to the support they need and keep them safe from harm.[30]

Likewise, the Safeguarding Minister, Victoria Atkins, stated that:

> I know that lockdown restrictions are especially difficult for those experiencing domestic abuse. Home should be a safe place, but for those confined with an abuser it is clearly not. The codeword scheme will offer a lifeline to all victims, ensuring they get urgent help in a safe and discreet way.[31]

It certainly seems that the introduction of this scheme was a very positive development as regards responding to domestic abuse in Northern Ireland, as in other parts of the UK, particularly in the context of the COVID-19 pandemic. For example, the Chief Executive of SafeLives, Suzanne Jacob, commented that:

> Victims of domestic abuse are experts in their own situation and it's survivors of abuse who first asked for this scheme. We need to give victims as many options as possible, including during the very tight restrictions of lockdown. The Ask for ANI scheme will provide a further vital lifeline for domestic abuse victims trapped by their perpetrators because of Covid. A trip to a participating shop or pharmacy might be a critical opportunity for someone to get the help they desperately need. We commend the government for listening to survivors and launching this scheme, and hope that more retailers take up the scheme so that victims across the country have a route to safety.[32]

Domestic Homicide Reviews

As was discussed in Chapter 3, section 9 of the Domestic Violence, Crime and Victims Act 2004 makes provision for the introduction of domestic homicide reviews. In July 2018, the Department of Justice had launched a consultation seeking views on a proposed model for the introduction of such reviews in Northern Ireland.[33] A summary of responses to the consultation was published in January 2019,[34] and respondents were unanimously in support of the introduction of domestic homicide reviews in Northern Ireland.

Domestic homicide reviews were subsequently introduced in this jurisdiction in December 2020. Three independent Chairs were appointed, one of whom leads each review to produce a report, with the support of a panel comprising various agencies, and also community and voluntary sector organisations. A decision on whether or not to commission a domestic homicide review is taken as soon as practicable and within six weeks of a death. The length of time needed for completion of such a review is dependent on the specifics of the case and on whether the review has to be paused due to ongoing criminal proceedings. As part of the review process, relevant information regarding the deceased person and their close family and friends is requested from various sources, such as statutory bodies, friends and family, and voluntary sector and community organisations. The Chair's report is then considered by a Senior Oversight Forum which is chaired by the Department of Justice and which comprises representatives from the PSNI, the Probation Board for Northern Ireland, and the Health and Social Care Board. Membership also includes one individual representing all of the Health and Social Care Trusts. The intention is that this multi-agency approach will ensure that any learning highlighted in the report can be shared in order to improve future outcomes.[35]

The introduction of domestic homicide reviews to Northern Ireland is certainly to be welcomed. The purpose of such reviews is to prevent the occurrence of future domestic homicides and to improve service responses for victims of domestic abuse. As the Justice Minister commented, 'Domestic Homicide Reviews will illuminate the past to make the future safer for those who may be at risk or who are being subjected to domestic abuse'.[36] The Chief Constable of the PSNI, Simon Byrne, stated upon the introduction of such reviews that the PSNI would

> work closely and collaboratively with our colleagues in the Department of Justice through the Domestic Homicide Review framework as a means to continually learn and do all we can to minimise the number of people who suffer Domestic Abuse in the future.[37]

Domestic Abuse and Civil Proceedings Act (Northern Ireland) 2021

As was discussed in Chapters 2 and 3, prior to the passing of the Domestic Abuse and Civil Proceedings Act (Northern Ireland) 2021, the legislative position as regards domestic abuse in Northern Ireland was problematic. Essentially, there was no specific offence of domestic abuse in this jurisdiction. Coercive control was not criminalised, a situation which failed to comply with relevant human rights standards. As was discussed in Chapter 3, steps had been taken towards rectifying this situation. In 2016 the Department of Justice had launched a public consultation on whether a specific offence of coercive and controlling behaviour should be enacted. Responses were generally in the affirmative, with respondents making the point that the introduction of such an offence would be a positive step which would clearly indicate that domestic abuse in all its forms would not be tolerated in society. Respondents were also of the view that the creation of a specific offence would give the police the opportunity to intervene at an early stage, thus potentially preventing domestic abuse from escalating.[38] Indeed, legislation criminalising coercive control was subsequently drafted for Northern Ireland, however unfortunately the passage of this stalled due to the suspension of the Northern Ireland Assembly from January 2017 until January 2020.[39] This meant that, until March 2021, Northern Ireland was the only jurisdiction within the UK and Ireland in which coercive control was not criminalised.

However, upon the restoration of the Northern Ireland Assembly in January 2020, securing the enactment of such legislation was a key priority of the Department of Justice[40] and on 31 March 2020 the Domestic Abuse and Family Proceedings Bill was introduced in the Assembly. This legislation subsequently received Royal Assent on 1 March 2021 as the Domestic Abuse and Civil Proceedings Act (Northern Ireland) 2021.[41] The passage of the legislation coincided with the first year of the COVID-19 pandemic and, as the Justice Minister, Naomi Long MLA, stated during Assembly debates on the legislation, the crucial importance of addressing the issue of domestic abuse became 'even more apparent during the current COVID-19 crisis'.[42] This factor may thus have contributed towards easing the passage of the Bill through the Assembly, and the effect of the pandemic on levels of domestic abuse arose several times during Assembly debates on the legislation. For example, the Justice Minister commented that:

> As we advise people to stay home, stay safe, save lives, we are also mindful that, for many in our community, home is not a safe place or a haven from harm. Instead, it is the very place where they are most vulnerable to abuse and to their abuser. Combined with physical distancing, which so often ends in social isolation, those already at risk have found themselves frequently without their most basic support networks or the temporary respite from

> abuse that being able to leave their home, even for a short time, might bring, compounding their vulnerability and the risk of harm. Whilst the current crisis has raised awareness of the plight of those who are victims of domestic abuse, it is imperative that our response is not temporary or fleeting, because domestic abuse is neither.[43]

Likewise, the Chair of the Justice Committee, Paul Givan MLA, stated that:

> When we consider the impact of COVID-19, the regulations that are in place and the restrictions that are being placed on people, we note an increased number of calls to the police about domestic abuse. We have clearly communicated a message that we are to stay at home, save lives and protect the NHS, but, for victims of domestic abuse, staying at home means to be abused and not to have the opportunity to escape that abuse, because there is a fear that, when they, out of necessity, cannot be in that environment, they somehow jeopardise the wider public good.[44]

Essentially, as Kellie Armstrong MLA stated:

> While (the legislation) was already very much needed…there has, unfortunately, been an increase in reports to the police of domestic abuse across Northern Ireland during the COVID-19 crisis. That is why the legislation is needed so quickly. People need to know that their abusers will be prosecuted and the conditions that need to be met in order to achieve a successful prosecution.[45]

Indeed, it is noteworthy that the provisions of the Bill relating to the domestic abuse offence were ultimately enacted with very little amendment.

The Explanatory and Financial Memorandum to the Bill stated that the introduction of an offence of domestic abuse would give effect ‘to the intention to improve the operation of the justice system by creating an offence that recognises the experience of victims, the repetitive nature of abusive behaviour and the potential cumulative effect of domestic abuse’.[46] It was intended that:

> By enabling a range of domestic abuse incidents, which take place over a period of time, to be prosecuted as a single course of behaviour within a new offence, the criminal law (would) better reflect how victims actually experience such abuse.[47]

Section 1 of the Domestic Abuse and Civil Proceedings Act (Northern Ireland) 2021 is entitled, 'the domestic abuse offence', and section 1(1) states that:

> A person ('A') commits an offence if –
>
> (a) A engages in a course of behaviour that is abusive of another person ('B'),
> (b) A and B are personally connected to each other at the time, and
> (c) both of the further conditions are met.

Under section 1(2), the further conditions are:

> (a) that a reasonable person would consider the course of behaviour to be likely to cause B to suffer physical or psychological harm, and
> (b) that A –
>   (i) intends the course of behaviour to cause B to suffer physical or psychological harm, or
>   (ii) is reckless as to whether the course of behaviour causes B to suffer physical or psychological harm.

The Financial and Explanatory Memorandum to the Bill stated that:

> The court would be entitled to take account of the circumstances of the case, for example any particular vulnerability of the partner/connected person, in considering whether the accused's behaviour would be likely to cause them to suffer physical or psychological harm.[48]

As regards section 1(2)(b)(ii), the Memorandum asserted that this condition could be met where, for instance, the defendant is persistently verbally abusive and demeaning, but claims that they did not intend their behaviour to result in harm.[49] Section 1(3) states that the references to 'psychological harm' include 'fear, alarm and distress'.

Section 3(1) asserts that the offence can be committed whether or not the behaviour in question in fact caused harm. As was referred to in Chapter 3, abusive behaviour (including psychological abuse) towards a partner or ex-partner was criminalised in Scotland under section 1 of the Domestic Abuse (Scotland) Act 2018, and the approach adopted in the 2021 Act mirrors that contained in section 1(2) and (3) and section 4(1) of the Domestic Abuse (Scotland) Act. As was also discussed in Chapter 3, coercive and controlling behaviour was criminalised in England and Wales under section 76 of the Serious Crime Act 2015. For an offence to be committed under this provision, the behaviour must have a 'serious effect' on the victim,[50] and the defendant must know or ought to have known that the behaviour would have such an effect.[51] According to section 76(5), the defendant 'ought to know' that which 'a reasonable person in possession of the same information would know'. Under section 76(4) the behaviour in question will be deemed to have had a 'serious effect' if it causes the victim to fear, on at least two occasions, that violence will be used against them,[52] or if it causes the victim serious alarm or distress which has a substantial adverse effect on their normal day-to-day activities.[53] Again as was referred to in Chapter 3, coercive control was criminalised in the Republic of Ireland under section 39 of the Domestic Violence Act 2018, and this provision uses a broadly similar approach to that of section 76 of the Serious Crime Act, in that according to section 39(1) of the Irish legislation, for an offence to be committed the defendant must 'knowingly' engage in the relevant behaviour, this behaviour must have 'a serious effect'[54] and it must be established that a reasonable person would consider the behaviour likely to have such an effect.[55] The term 'knowingly' is not however further defined. Under section 39(2), the behaviour will be deemed to have had 'a serious effect' if it causes the victim 'to fear that violence will be used against him or her',[56] or causes the victim 'serious alarm or distress that has a substantial adverse impact on his or her usual day-to-day activities'.[57] Unlike section 76(4)(a) of the Serious Crime Act, there is no requirement that the victim has feared that violence will be used against them 'on at least two occasions'. The approach adopted by the Northern Irish legislation, as with the Scottish Act, is thus broader than that adopted by section 76 of the Serious Crime Act and section 39 of the Republic of Ireland's Domestic Violence Act.

Also, under the Northern Irish and Scottish Acts, for an offence to be committed, there is no need to prove that the behaviour in question actually caused harm, but only that the behaviour was likely to cause physical or psychological harm, and that the defendant intended to cause such harm or was reckless as to whether such harm was caused. As the Justice Minister commented during debates in the Assembly on the Northern Irish Bill, this reflects 'the resilience of the victim or that, for many, abusive behaviour has effectively become normalised'.[58] Herring remarks in respect of the Scottish legislation that, 'This approach has some benefits as it allows for a prosecution in cases where the victim is unwilling or reluctant to give evidence and so proof of the impact on them is difficult'.[59] As Bishop and Bettinson discuss, the need to prove that serious harm has occurred has caused problems in establishing successful prosecutions under section 76 of the Serious Crime Act,[60] and so it appears meritorious that this requirement has not been adopted under the Northern Irish legislation.

Section 2(2) of the 2021 Act focuses on the meaning of 'abusive' and asserts that:

> Behaviour that is abusive of B includes (in particular) –
>
> (a) behaviour directed at B that is violent,
> (b) behaviour directed at B that is threatening,
> (c) behaviour directed at B, at a child of B or at someone else that –
>   (i) has as its purpose (or among its purposes) one or more of the relevant effects, or
>   (ii) would be considered by a reasonable person to be likely to have one or more of the relevant effects.

According to section 2(3), the 'relevant effects' referred to above are:

> (a) making B dependent on, or subordinate to, A,
> (b) isolating B from friends, family members or other sources of social interaction or support,
> (c) controlling, regulating or monitoring B's day-to-day activities,
> (d) depriving B of, or restricting B's, freedom of action,
> (e) making B feel frightened, humiliated, degraded, punished or intimidated.

The Explanatory and Financial Memorandum stated that the inclusion of the relevant effects that can indicate that behaviour is abusive was 'intended to ensure that, for example, psychological abuse, or controlling or coercive behaviour that could not currently be prosecuted under existing offences, falls within the definition of abusive behaviour (as well as violent or threatening behaviour)'.[61] During Assembly debates on the Bill, the Justice Minister, Naomi Long, commented that, 'The effects of the abusive behaviour set out in the Bill are deliberately broad, recognising that each person's experience will be different'.[62] Section 3 clarifies that the offence can be committed 'whether or not A's behaviour actually causes B to suffer harm of the sort referred to in section 1(2)',[63] and that 'A's behaviour can be abusive of B by virtue of section 2(2)(c) whether or not A's behaviour actually has one or more of the relevant effects set out in section 2(3)'.[64]

Section 4(2) of the 2021 Act addresses the meaning of 'behaviour' and states that:

> Behaviour is behaviour of any kind, including (for example) –
>
> (a) saying or otherwise communicating something as well as doing something,
> (b) intentionally failing –
>   (i) to do something, or
>   (ii) to say or otherwise communicate something.

The Explanatory and Financial Memorandum stated that, 'This could include, for example, a failure to pass on times and dates of appointments or social occasions, a failure to feed a family pet or a failure to speak to or communicate with an individual'.[65] Under section 4(3),

> Behaviour is directed at a person if it is directed at the person in any way, including (for example) –
>
> (a) through –
>   (i) conduct relating to the person's ability to acquire, use or maintain money or other property or the person's ability to obtain goods or services, or
>   (ii) other conduct concerning or towards property, or
> (b) by making use of a third party,
>
> as well as in a personal or direct manner.

In relation to section 4(3)(a), the Explanatory and Financial Memorandum clarified that such conduct could be with regard to shared property or property belonging to parents, and that property would include pets or other animals whether belonging to the victim or to others.[66] As regards section 4(3)(b), the Memorandum asserted that the behaviour in question could involve, for example, using a third party to spy on or report on the victim's activities.[67] According to section 4(4), 'A course of behaviour involves behaviour on at least two occasions'.

Section 5(2) states that the parties are 'personally connected' if they are, or have been, married to each other[68] or civil partners of each other;[69] they are living together, or have lived together, as if spouses of each other;[70] they are, or have been, otherwise in an intimate personal relationship with each other;[71] or they are members of the same family.[72] According to section 5(3), being 'members of the same family' encompasses B being A's parent, grandparent, child, grandchild, sister or brother. The requirement for a personal connection between the parties is likewise contained in section 76(1)(b) of the Serious Crime Act. Although the definition of 'personally connected' found in section 76(2) and (6) of the latter is not identical to that contained in section 5 of the Northern Irish legislation, under both Acts the relevant offences can pertain in circumstances beyond those in which the parties are intimate partners. During Assembly debates on the Northern Irish legislation, the Justice Minister commented that, 'the devastating impact of familial domestic abuse on victims should not be underestimated and should be captured by this new offence'.[73] This differs significantly from the approach taken in the Scottish legislation. Under section 1(1) of the Domestic Abuse (Scotland) Act, the offence in question is limited to a course of behaviour which is abusive of the defendant's partner or ex-partner. Similarly, the offence of coercive control contained in the Republic of Ireland's Domestic Violence Act must be committed against a 'relevant person',[74] with this phrase being defined as meaning the spouse or civil partner of the defendant or a person who is or was in an intimate relationship with the defendant.[75] As Cairns remarks:

> On the one hand, it can be argued that there is a stronger case for narrowness in the interests of capturing effectively the distinct moral wrong of domestic abuse (which has been said to arise from its systematic nature and the abuse of trust involved) and avoiding overcriminalisation. On the other hand, it can be argued that if individuals other than partners or ex-partners are also capable of experiencing systematic abuse that erodes their freedom and has a significant impact on their daily lives, then the offence should be more widely available to ensure that these individuals are not arbitrarily denied legal protection based on relationship status.[76]

In addition, it is noteworthy that the definition of 'personally connected' contained in section 5(2) of the Northern Irish legislation includes those who have lived together as if spouses of each other.

Ex-partners are also included under section 1(1) of the Scottish legislation and section 39(4) of the Republic of Ireland's legislation, however they were not originally encompassed under section 76 of the Serious Crime Act. Section 76 has however now been amended by section 68 of the Domestic Abuse Act 2021 to include ex-partners. Respondents to the Department of Justice's 2016 consultation were of the opinion that a domestic abuse offence should encapsulate situations in which ex-partners are continuing to use coercive control even after separation,[77] and it appears that such an approach is to be welcomed. As Cairns comments, 'Research has consistently shown that those in abusive relationships are at greatest risk of serious abuse when they are trying to leave their partner or when recently separated'.[78] Also, child contact arrangements can provide opportunities for former partners to engage in abuse.[79]

Under section 8(1) of the 2021 Act, the domestic abuse offence is aggravated if the victim was under the age of 18 at the time when the offence was committed. There is no equivalent provision in the relevant legislation of any of the other jurisdictions in the UK and Ireland, and the inclusion of this provision in the 2021 Act is meritorious.

In addition, under section 9(1), the offence is aggravated if a relevant child is involved, for instance if a child witnessed the offence taking place. An equivalent provision is found in section 5 of the Domestic Abuse (Scotland) Act, and the fact that this is replicated in the 2021 Act is to be welcomed, given the harm that can be caused to children by exposure to domestic abuse.[80] By contrast, neither section 39 of the Republic of Ireland's Domestic Violence Act nor section 76 of the Serious Crime Act encompass such a provision. According to section 9(2) of the 2021 Act 'involving a relevant child' occurs if

(a) at any time in the commission of the offence –
    (i) A directed, or threatened to direct, behaviour at the child, or
    (ii) A made use of the child in directing behaviour at B, or
(b) the child saw or heard, or was present during, an incident of behaviour which A directed at B as part of the course of behaviour, or
(c) a reasonable person would consider the course of behaviour, or an incident of A's behaviour that forms part of the course of behaviour, to be likely to adversely affect the child.

According to section 9(8)(a), a 'relevant child' is defined as being a person under the age of 18 who is not A or B. During Assembly debates on the Bill, the Justice Minister commented that, 'We...know that witnessing domestic abuse is devastating for children and can have a long-lasting impact on their well-being...I consider these provisions essential in recognising the damaging effect that domestic abuse can have on children'.[81] Section 9(3) was not included in the provisions of the Bill as introduced, but was added with the aim of making it clear that in order for the offence to be aggravated due to the involvement of a child, there does not need to be any evidence that the child in question had ever had any awareness or understanding of A's behaviour,[82] or had ever been adversely affected by this behaviour.[83] The Committee for Justice reported that generally these aggravator clauses were welcomed by the organisations which submitted evidence in relation to the Bill.[84]

However, according to section 11(1) of the Northern Irish legislation, A does not commit the domestic abuse offence in relation to B by engaging in behaviour that is abusive of B at a time when B is under the age of 16 and A has responsibility for B. No such provision is contained in the Irish or Scottish legislation, as such situations do not come within the scope of these Acts. An equivalent provision is nevertheless contained in section 76(3) of the Serious Crime Act. According to the Statutory Guidance to the latter, the rationale for the inclusion of this provision was that abusive behaviour in such circumstances was already covered by other aspects of the criminal law.[85] Likewise, the Statutory Guidance issued by the Department of Justice in February 2022 in relation to the 2021 Act states that such abuse should be dealt with under child protection legislation, including the child cruelty offence found in section 20 of the Children and Young Person Act (Northern Ireland) 1968 which was amended by section 21 of the 2021 Act to include expressly ill-treatment which is non-physical.[86]

In addition, under section 12(1) of the 2021 Act, 'it is a defence for A to show that the course of behaviour was reasonable in the particular circumstances'. The Committee for Justice was of the view that, 'given the scope of the offence and the wide personal connection, the Clause provides a necessary balance to the Bill'.[87] However, the Committee proceeded to assert that it expected the Department of Justice 'to closely monitor the use of this defence', and that if there is 'any indication that the defence is being manipulated by perpetrators or is providing a "loophole" for abusive behaviour the Department must take swift action to provide a remedy'.[88] The Statutory Guidance states that this defence constitutes 'an important safeguard to ensure that those acting in the best interests of others are not criminalised', however it is intended that the defence would only be used in very limited circumstances.[89] The

Statutory Guidance suggests that this defence could apply, for example, if an individual has a partner with an alcohol or gambling addiction and for that reason prevents them from associating with certain people or having control of the household finances.[90]

A similar defence is contained in section 6 of the Domestic Abuse (Scotland) Act. A 'reasonableness' defence is also found in section 76(8) of the Serious Crime Act, although for this defence to be applicable, not only must the behaviour in question be 'in all the circumstances reasonable',[91] but the defendant must demonstrate that he or she was acting in the best interests of the person against whom the behaviour is exerted.[92] In addition, it is stated that this defence cannot be used in relation to behaviour that causes fear of violence.[93] No such 'reasonableness' defence is found in section 39 of the Republic of Ireland's Domestic Violence Act.

Under section 14 of the 2021 Act, a person who commits the domestic abuse offence is liable, on summary conviction, to imprisonment for a term not exceeding 12 months or a fine (or both);[94] or, on conviction on indictment, to imprisonment for a term not exceeding 14 years or a fine (or both).[95] This is identical to the penalties which may be imposed for committing an offence under section 1 of the Domestic Abuse (Scotland) Act. By contrast, a person who commits an offence under section 76 of the Serious Crime Act or section 39 of the Republic of Ireland's Domestic Violence Act is liable on conviction on indictment to a term of imprisonment of only five years.[96] Bishop comments in respect of the section 76 offence that, 'As it carries a maximum sentence of only five years imprisonment, there is…an inference that it is less serious in nature than direct physical violence'.[97] Bishop remarks that coercive control may cause extreme psychological harm, which can result in victims taking their own lives, and proceeds to state that,

> if coercion and control were viewed along the same lines as the spectrum of criminal offences against the person, arguably at its very peak, it is as serious as an offence of grievous bodily harm with intent and thus should carry the same maximum sentence of life imprisonment.[98]

A number of respondents to the Department of Justice's public consultation of February 2016 stressed 'the need for a strong sentencing regime with the offence, to reflect the seriousness of domestic abuse/coercive and controlling behaviour and the significant adverse impact this type of abuse has on victims'.[99] It is welcome that the Northern

Ireland Assembly took note of such responses and chose to follow the approach of the Scottish legislation by adopting a maximum term of imprisonment of 14 years for commission of the new domestic abuse offence. During Assembly debates on the Bill, the Justice Minister remarked that, 'It is...essential that we set a penalty that corresponds with the seriousness of the offence'.[100] As stated in the Explanatory and Financial Memorandum, 'The nature of the penalties is intended to reflect the cumulative nature of the offence over time, that it may cover both physical and psychological abuse and also the intimate and trusting nature of the relationships involved'.[101] In its consideration of the Bill, the Committee for Justice asserted that:

> the penalties demonstrate the seriousness with which the crime of domestic violence and abuse is viewed and sends a message to the perpetrators, the victims and the general public in Northern Ireland that such crimes are not acceptable and will not be tolerated.[102]

However, as Bettinson and Robson remark:

> a new offence alone will not improve criminal justice responses to domestic abuse; police, prosecutorial authorities and the courts interpret the law, therefore success in any legal jurisdiction will be based upon ongoing education of the public and specialist training of criminal justice personnel.[103]

Problems have arisen in relation to the implementation of offences of coercive control. As Bettinson and Robson comment, 'The discrepancy between the number of prosecutions and police recorded offences suggests that the prosecution authorities are facing difficulties bringing cases of coercive control before the courts',[104] and such problems may also emerge regarding the implementation of the domestic abuse offence in Northern Ireland. Such difficulties may manifest in particular in cases in which the victim does not wish to give evidence in court, a situation which may arise if, for example, the victim wishes to continue the relationship, distrusts the court process or fears retaliation from the perpetrator.[105] Essentially,

> The nature of oral evidence in these cases is that it exposes the victim to public scrutiny of their lifestyle, intimate relationships and decision making. A victim may be unwilling to expose themselves to this examination having been humiliated by the perpetrator and experiencing feelings of shame and embarrassment. It is

> also difficult to discuss the harm when it involves activities which are, on the face of it, not recognisably criminal as the prospects of success may be perceived as low; this is particularly true where the tactics used are non-physical.[106]

However, as Bettinson and Robson remark in relation to section 76 of the Serious Crime Act, 'The difficulty in prosecuting the s.76 offence without the victim's testimony is the nature of the behaviour criminalised means that it is generally performed in private and cannot be easily evidenced through alternative means'.[107]

The Statutory Guidance produced by the Department of Justice in relation to the 2021 Act states that when police officers are called to incidents involving individuals who are personally connected, domestic abuse should always be considered as a potential factor.[108] The Guidance also emphasises the 'need to build trust with individuals, provide a tailored response and advise those affected about support services'.[109] It is important that police officers establish a good rapport with the victim, as if an incident is handled effectively and sympathetically, the victim is more likely to have the confidence to call the police again if the situation recurs.[110] In terms of gathering evidence, the Guidance states that police should focus on establishing a course of behaviour for the domestic abuse offence across different types of evidence. Much of this will be evidence of the victim and abuser's day-to-day living and interaction. The Guidance suggests a very wide range of types of evidence which may be helpful, such as the victim's account to police of what happened; records of communication between the victim and abuser such as phone records, emails or text messages; evidence of abuse over the internet, digital technology and social media platforms; audio or visual recordings of interaction between the victim and suspect such as CCTV or body-worn video footage; local enquiries of neighbours; witness testimony from family and friends; diaries kept by, for example, the victim or children; records of lifestyle, including photographic evidence; evidence of isolation such as lack of contact with family and friends; records of interaction with services which show the suspect having a dominant role, such as always accompanying the victim to medical or banking appointments without good reason; bank records demonstrating restricted financial management; and medical evidence including records of visits to a doctor or to a hospital out-patients' clinic or casualty department. If a victim is unwilling to engage with police or give evidence, the Guidance emphasises that officers should still take steps to build a case for a potential prosecution; and if a victim asks the police not to proceed any further with a case, this will not mean automatically that the case will be stopped.[111]

In addition, steps have been taken in the 2021 Act to assist complainants in giving evidence in cases involving the domestic abuse offence. Section 23 of the Act amends article 5 of the Criminal Evidence (Northern Ireland) Order 1999 to make such complainants eligible for special measures when giving evidence. These special measures may include screening the complainant from the accused;[112] giving evidence by means of a live link;[113] giving evidence in private;[114] or video recording the complainant's evidence in chief,[115] cross-examination or re-examination.[116] Also, section 24 of the 2021 Act inserts a new article 22A into the 1999 Order, asserting that no person charged with an offence involving domestic abuse may cross-examine the complainant in person. During Assembly debates, the Justice Minister remarked in relation to these provisions that:

> Shamefully, some abusers also seek to use the criminal justice system itself to further victimise their partner, ex-partner or family member. For that reason, the Bill includes safeguards to prevent an abuser using the criminal justice process to further exert control and influence over a victim. These provisions should help to minimise the trauma for the victim, while ensuring that the proper administration of justice is achieved…Together, I believe that the provisions will help victims to give the best evidence that they can in court, and also reduce the number of victims disengaging from the criminal justice system.[117]

Similarly, the Chairperson of the Committee for Justice, Paul Givan, commented that, 'It is essential to ensure that victims of domestic abuse are not revictimised by contact with the criminal justice process and that victims have their needs taken into account at appropriate points in the process'.[118]

The creation of a domestic abuse offence for Northern Ireland is an immensely positive development. The introduction of this offence brings Northern Ireland into line with the other jurisdictions within the UK and Ireland, and also with human rights standards, in terms of criminalising coercive and controlling behaviour. The fact that the very clear deficiency in Northern Ireland's legislative response to domestic abuse has now been addressed is greatly to be welcomed. Although this development was certainly overdue, it is true that being the final jurisdiction within the UK and Ireland, to criminalise such behaviour has enabled Northern Ireland's approach to be informed by the earlier legislation enacted in the other jurisdictions and, to some degree, has allowed Northern Ireland to 'cherry-pick' the most positive aspects of the approaches of these jurisdictions. As the Justice Minister stated during Assembly debates on the Bill, 'Importantly, as part of our deliberations, we...considered offences in other jurisdictions relating to controlling and coercive behaviour, including what is often perceived as the Scottish gold standard'.[119]

In addition, there are aspects of Northern Ireland's domestic abuse offence which differ from the approaches of any of the other jurisdictions within the UK and Ireland. For instance, there is no equivalent provision in the relevant legislation in any of the other jurisdictions to section 8(1) of the Northern Irish Act, under which the domestic abuse offence is aggravated if the victim was under the age of 18 at the time when the offence was committed. The inclusion of this provision in the 2021 Act is certainly meritorious.

It is also important to note that under section 15 of the 2021 Act, a charge relating to any offence other than the new domestic abuse offence may be regarded as 'aggravated' by reason of involving domestic abuse, thereby resulting in an increased sentence if a conviction ensues. Under section 16, three conditions must be met for an offence committed by a person ('A') to be aggravated in this manner. These conditions are; firstly, that a reasonable person would consider the commission of the offence by A to be likely to cause another person ('B') to suffer physical or psychological harm;[120] secondly, that A intends the commission of the offence to cause physical or psychological harm to B, or is reckless as to whether the commission of the offence causes such harm;[121] and thirdly, that A and B are personally connected.[122] As with the domestic abuse offence, according to section 18 the parties are regarded as being 'personally connected' if they are, or have been, married to each other[123] or civil partners of each other;[124] they are living together, or have lived together, as if spouses of each other;[125] they are, or have been, otherwise in an intimate personal relationship with each other;[126] or they are members of the same family[127] which includes B being A's parent, grandparent, child, grandchild, sister or brother.[128] Interestingly, under section 16(3)(a) an offence can be aggravated whether or not the offence was actually committed against B. As noted in the Explanatory and Financial Memorandum, the domestic abuse aggravator could be attached if, for example, the accused committed criminal damage against a friend of their partner with the intention of thereby causing psychological harm to their partner.[129] An offence can also be aggravated whether or not the commission of that offence actually caused B to suffer harm.[130] If both the charge and the aggravation are proved, under section 15(4), the court must:

(a) state on conviction that the offence is aggravated by reason of involving domestic abuse,
(b) record the conviction in a way that shows that the offence is so aggravated,
(c) in determining the appropriate sentence, treat the fact that the offence is so aggravated as a factor that increases the seriousness of the offence, and
(d) in imposing sentence, explain how the fact that the offence is so aggravated affects the sentence imposed.

Section 23 makes complainants eligible for special measures when giving evidence in cases involving offences to which the domestic abuse aggravator is attached.

The domestic abuse aggravator provisions constitute a very valuable part of the 2021 Act, and the Committee for Justice reported that there was widespread support for these provisions in the evidence received on the Bill.[131] The domestic abuse aggravator has the potential to apply to a wide range of offences, and the Statutory Guidance suggests that the most common types of offences to which the aggravator could be attached include criminal damage, assault, threats to damage property and threats to kill. For example, if someone deliberately caused criminal damage to their partner's car, the domestic abuse aggravator could be attached to the charge of criminal damage.[132] As was discussed in Chapter 2, historically the fact that a crime was committed in a domestic context was frequently viewed as a factor which made it less serious. For example, an assault committed between strangers would often have been treated more seriously than an assault by one partner against another.[133] The value of the principle now being encapsulated in legislation that domestic abuse should be seen as an aggravating factor, as opposed to a mitigation, should not therefore be underestimated.

In England and Wales, there is no statutory domestic abuse aggravator, although the Sentencing Council[134] has issued guidelines stating that offending behaviour is more serious in a domestic context due to the violation of trust and security that is involved.[135] Nevertheless it is arguably meritorious that Northern Ireland has chosen to legislate for a domestic abuse aggravator, as this clearly conveys to victims, perpetrators and the public more broadly that domestic abuse is a serious matter which will not be tolerated by the criminal justice system.

Northern Ireland's statutory domestic abuse aggravator is not however the first of its kind to be implemented within the UK and Ireland. In Scotland, section 1 of the Abusive Behaviour and Sexual Harm (Scotland) Act 2016 came into force in April 2017. Under this provision, an offence is aggravated if in committing the offence, the perpetrator intends to cause their partner or ex-partner to suffer physical or psychological harm;[136] or in the case of an offence committed against the partner or ex-partner, the perpetrator is reckless as to whether such harm is caused.[137] If the offence and the aggravation are proved, the court must take the aggravation into account when determining the appropriate sentence.[138] In the Republic of Ireland, section 40 of the Domestic Violence Act 2018 provides that where a court is determining the sentence in relation to certain offences, the fact that the offence was committed by the perpetrator against their spouse or civil partner or against someone with whom they were in an intimate relationship, should be treated as an aggravating factor. However, although the aggravator provisions in Scotland and the Republic of Ireland came into effect substantially earlier than those in Northern Ireland, it is notable that Northern Ireland's provisions are significantly broader than those of the other jurisdictions. The provisions in Scotland and the Republic of Ireland relate only to partners and ex-partners, whereas Northern Ireland's aggravator provisions encompass a wider range of family relationships. Also, for an offence to be aggravated in the Republic of Ireland, the offence must be committed against a partner or ex-partner; whereas in Northern Ireland an offence can be aggravated even if it was not actually committed against the person to whom the perpetrator is personally connected. In addition, the aggravator provision in the Republic of Ireland can be used only in relation to particular offences such as a range of offences against the person, rape, sexual assault and aggravated sexual assault.[139] By contrast, the aggravator provisions in Northern Ireland can be used as regards any offence, apart from the new domestic abuse offence itself. The fact that Northern Ireland has chosen to adopt the most expansive approach is arguably advantageous, as this allows the aggravator provisions to be used in the widest range of cases.

The provisions of the 2021 Act came into operation on 21 February 2022.[140] The new domestic abuse offence and the new domestic abuse aggravator provisions together constitute a milestone in the response of the criminal justice system in Northern Ireland to domestic abuse. Far from a domestic abuse context being seen as lessening the seriousness of an offence, it is now very firmly established that not only is domestic abuse a criminal offence in itself, but it is also to be viewed as increasing the seriousness of other offences in terms of sentencing. It will doubtless take some time for a substantial body of jurisprudence to be built up in relation to either the domestic abuse offence or the domestic abuse aggravator provision. Nevertheless, it is to be hoped that both will contribute effectively to increased protection for victims of domestic abuse in Northern Ireland.

Protection from Stalking Act (Northern Ireland) 2022

However, although the enactment of the Domestic Abuse and Civil Proceedings Act was certainly a major step forward as regards improving Northern Ireland's legislative response to domestic abuse, further measures were still necessary. As was discussed in Chapter 3, it has been found that most stalking offences are committed by abusive ex-partners.[141] An effective approach to addressing domestic abuse should therefore encompass a sufficient response to stalking. As was noted in Chapter 3, specific offences of stalking were enacted in Scotland in 2010[142] and in England and Wales in 2012.[143] However, until the enactment of the Protection from Stalking Act (Northern Ireland) 2022, there was no specific offence of stalking in Northern Ireland. Instead, the more general offences of harassment as found in article 4 of the Protection from Harassment (Northern Ireland) Order 1997 and putting people in fear of violence as found in article 6 of the Order had to be relied upon in cases involving stalking. As with the enactment of legislation criminalising coercive control, again Northern Ireland's legislative response was 'lagging behind' that of the rest of the UK, and in this case even more markedly, given that specific offences of stalking had been enacted as far back as 2010 in Scotland and 2012 in England and Wales.

As was also discussed in Chapter 3, in November 2018, the Department of Justice had launched a public consultation on the creation of a new offence of stalking in Northern Ireland. Of all respondents to the consultation, 93 per cent were of the view that the current legislative position was insufficient,[144] and the Department stated that it would be recommending to an incoming Justice Minister that a stalking bill containing provisions to give effect to the introduction of a new specific offence of stalking and to stalking protection orders, be developed for introduction to a future Assembly.[145] Such legislation was indeed introduced to the Assembly on 18 January 2021, and was enacted into law on 26 April 2022.

Under section 1(1) of the Protection from Stalking Act (Northern Ireland) 2022, a new offence of stalking is created. This offence is committed if a person (A) engages in a course of conduct that causes another person (B) to suffer fear, alarm or substantial distress or is such that a reasonable person, or a reasonable person who has any particular knowledge of B that A has, would consider to be likely to cause them to suffer fear, alarm or substantial distress. However, under section 1(2), in order for the offence to be committed, A must have either intended the conduct to cause fear, alarm or substantial distress, or ought in the circumstances to have known that this effect would have been caused.

Under section 1(4), the meaning of 'conduct' is defined as following B or any other person; contacting, or attempting to contact, B or any other person by any means; publishing any statement or other material relating or purporting to relate to B or to any other person, or purporting to originate from B or from any other person; monitoring the use by B or by any other person of the internet, email or any other form of electronic communication; entering any premises; loitering in any place; interfering with any property in the possession of B or of any other person; giving anything to B or to any other person or leaving anything where it may be found by, given to or brought to the attention of B or any other person; watching or spying on B or any other person; or acting in any other way that a reasonable person, or a reasonable person who has any particular knowledge of B that A has, would expect would cause B to suffer fear, alarm or substantial distress. A 'course of conduct' is defined as meaning conduct on two or more occasions, and 'substantial distress' is defined as distress which has a substantial adverse effect on B's day to day activities.

According to section 1(6), the maximum penalty for commission of the stalking offence is, on summary conviction, 12 months of imprisonment or a fine or both. The maximum penalty on conviction on indictment is a term of imprisonment of up to ten years or a fine or both.

Under section 2(1) of the Act, an offence of threatening or abusive behaviour is also created. This offence is committed where a person (A) behaves in a threatening or abusive manner and the behaviour would be likely to cause a reasonable person to suffer fear and alarm; and A intends the behaviour to have this effect or is reckless as to whether it does so. According to section 2(3), the behaviour in question can be of any type including, in particular, things said or otherwise communicated as well as actions. The behaviour can consist of a single act or omission or a course of conduct. Under section 2(4) of the Act, the maximum penalty on summary conviction of the offence of threatening or abusive behaviour is 12 months of imprisonment or a fine or both. The maximum penalty on conviction on indictment is a term of imprisonment of up to five years or a fine or both.

Sections 6–17 of the Act provide for the introduction of Stalking Protection Orders. Such an order can prohibit a person from carrying out acts associated with stalking, such as entering certain locations where the victim resides or frequently visits, contacting the victim by any means or approaching the victim. A Stalking Protection Order can also impose requirements such as attending a perpetrator intervention programme.[146] Under these provisions, the PSNI may apply to the court for such an order if it appears that a person has carried out acts associated with stalking and poses a risk associated with stalking, and that there is reasonable cause to believe that an order is necessary to protect another person from this risk.[147]

It is hoped that by later in 2022 the new offences will come into operation and Stalking Protection Orders will begin to be available. The Justice Minister, Naomi Long, has commented that,

> The delivery of this new legislation offers greater protection in our communities and its passing will be of great significance to anyone affected by stalking...This new legislation will play a crucial part in generating confidence in victims to come forward and report to the police in the knowledge that they will receive the support and protections they need and deserve to feel safe.[148]

Legislation on Non-fatal Strangulation

In July 2021, the Department of Justice launched a public consultation on the issue of non-fatal strangulation.[149] This consultation related to the recommendation which had been made by Criminal Justice Inspection Northern Ireland (CJINI) in its 2019 report that the Department should review how potential inadequacies in current legislation regarding choking or strangulation could be addressed. As noted below, in its 2021 follow-up report, CJINI had considered this recommendation to be only partially achieved, however the public consultation served to implement further the recommendation.[150]

Section 21 of the Offences Against the Person Act 1861 states that,

> Whosoever shall, by any means whatsoever, attempt to choke, suffocate, or strangle any other person, or shall by any means calculated to choke, suffocate, or strangle, attempt to render any other person insensible, unconscious, or incapable of resistance, with intent in any of such cases thereby to enable himself or any other person to

> commit, or with intent in any of such cases thereby to assist any other person in committing, any indictable offence, shall be guilty of felony, and being convicted thereof shall be liable to be kept in penal servitude for life.

This offence can only be tried in the Crown Court, and the maximum sentence is life imprisonment. However, the requirement that the offence can only be prosecuted if there is evidence of intention to commit another indictable offence may be problematic. In cases in which a charge of strangulation cannot be brought, alternative charges, such as assault or unlawful detention, may be used and the defendant may be tried in the Magistrates' Court. However, in such instances, the offence charged may not reflect the harm that has been caused, and the available sentence may not address all of the circumstances involved. For instance, usually the maximum sentence which can be imposed in the Magistrates' Court is six months' imprisonment. In the Crown Court, the maximum sentence for assault occasioning actual bodily harm is seven years' imprisonment, and for indictable common assault the maximum sentence is two years.[151]

In England and Wales, in April 2021 section 70 of the Domestic Abuse Act added a new offence of strangulation or suffocation to the Serious Crime Act 2015. Under the new section 75A(1) of the 2015 Act, the offence is constituted where a person intentionally strangles another or carries out any other act that affects their ability to breathe and which constitutes battery. Provided intentionally or recklessly inflicted serious harm does not result,[152] it is a defence for a person to show that the other person consented to the strangulation.[153] 'Serious harm' is defined as grievous bodily harm or wounding, within the meaning of section 18 of the Offences Against the Person Act, or actual bodily harm, within the meaning of section 47 of that Act.[154] The offence may be tried in a Magistrates' Court, in which case the maximum penalty imposed would be six months' imprisonment, or in the Crown Court, where the maximum penalty would be five years' imprisonment.[155]

A summary of responses to the Department of Justice consultation was published in November 2021,[156] and the overwhelming majority of respondents were of the view that the current law was not sufficient. Responses demonstrated a strong preference for the creation of a new stand-alone offence of non-fatal strangulation, in order to ensure clarity for victims, police, legal professionals and perpetrators; to increase protection for victims; and to demonstrate the extent and seriousness of the issue. In the summary of responses document, the

Justice Minister expressed her agreement that a new stand-alone offence should be created, with appropriate definitions and penalties, and stated that as well as allowing recognition by the criminal justice system of the specific nature of strangulation, this would pave the way for awareness raising and send an important public message as to the seriousness of the offence. The Justice Minister also agreed with the majority of respondents to the consultation that the new offence should be triable in both the Magistrates' Court and the Crown Court, with a maximum penalty in the Magistrates' Court of two years' imprisonment, and a maximum sentence in the Crown Court of 14 years' imprisonment. It was also stated by the majority of respondents, and agreed by the Minister, that expenditure would be needed on a programme of education to increase awareness of the problems associated with non-fatal strangulation.

An offence of non-fatal strangulation or asphyxiation was subsequently enacted in April 2022 under section 28 of the Justice (Sexual Offences and Trafficking Victims) Act (Northern Ireland) 2022. Under this provision, a person ('A') will commit an offence if two conditions are met.[157] These are, firstly, that A intentionally applies pressure on or to the throat or neck of another person ('B'), or does something else to B amounting to battery;[158] and secondly, that A intends the act to affect B's ability to breathe or the flow of blood to B's brain, or is reckless as to whether the act does so.[159] It is a defence to show that B consented to A's act, but the defence is not available if B suffers serious harm as a result of A's act, and A intended the act to cause B to suffer serious harm, or was reckless as to such harm was caused.[160] 'Serious harm' is defined as grievous bodily harm or wounding, within the meaning of section 18 of the Offences Against the Person Act, or actual bodily harm, within the meaning of section 47 of that Act.[161] A person who commits the offence is liable on conviction in the Magistrates' Court, to imprisonment for a term of up to two years, or a fine, or both; or on conviction in the Crown Court, to imprisonment for a term of up to 14 years, or a fine, or both.[162]

Criminal Justice Inspection Northern Ireland Follow-Up Report – April 2021

The enactment of the domestic abuse offence certainly constituted a very important development in relation to Northern Ireland's criminal justice response to this issue. The passing of the Protection from Stalking Act is also meritorious, as is the creation of an offence of non-fatal strangulation. However, it must not be forgotten that legislation in itself is insufficient as regards addressing domestic abuse. In April 2021 a follow-up review was published in respect of the 2019 report by CJINI on the handling of domestic abuse cases by the criminal justice system.[163] As was discussed in Chapter 3, seven recommendations had been made in the 2019 report; however, the follow-up review found that only one of these had been implemented, whilst four had been only partially achieved and two not implemented.

The first recommendation from the 2019 report had been that:

> The Police Service of Northern Ireland should develop an action plan, within six months of this report, to further develop the approach to dealing with cases of domestic violence and abuse and address the issues highlighted in relation to:
>
> - the training and development of new recruits and first responders in the areas of harassment, stalking and coercive and controlling behaviour; and
> - the risk assessment practices in cases of domestic violence and abuse.[164]

CJINI in its 2021 follow-up review noted that the PSNI were developing training to be implemented alongside the introduction of the Domestic Abuse and Civil Proceedings Act (Northern Ireland) 2021. This training was to include four phases: understanding coercive and controlling behaviour; investigative standards; pathways to support; and legislation. It was intended that 3,000–4,000 police officers and staff would be trained, including frontline police officers, custody officers and call handlers. It was planned that the quality assurance of the training would be managed by an internal police domestic abuse working group.[165]

In relation to risk assessment procedures, the Public Protection notification system had been introduced in November 2020. This had resulted in improvements to the process of submitting DASH (Domestic Abuse, Stalking and Harassment) forms to the PSNI's records management system and assisted police officers in assessing evidence collected through the DASH form in order to make decisions regarding assessment gradings. The PSNI were also developing work to focus on repeat victims and repeat perpetrators during 2021–2022. Changes to the information which was required to be provided by the PSNI to the PPS had included the addition of the outcome of the DASH form (that is, whether the victim was assessed to be at standard, moderate or high risk), as well as a requirement to include a domestic history if there had been prior domestic incidents between either the suspect and victim, or the suspect and other victims previously. Nevertheless, CJINI remained concerned that there was the potential for delays in decision-making or for important information to be missed, if the PPS had to make a further request for information that was included in the initial DASH form but which was not provided to them. CJINI thus encouraged the PSNI and the PPS to work together to make the sharing of electronic DASH forms possible, in order to ensure improved decision-making by the PPS and a reduction in avoidable delay. CJINI therefore concluded that this recommendation had been partially achieved.[166]

The second recommendation from the 2019 report had been that:

> The Police Service of Northern Ireland and Multi-Agency Risk Assessment Conference (MARAC) Operational Board should develop an action plan, within six months of this report, to further develop the multi-agency safeguarding arrangements for cases of domestic violence and abuse in Northern Ireland.[167]

CJINI accepted that some work has been undertaken in respect of this recommendation, but were of the view that progress seemed to be slow. It was recognised that agencies involved had been significantly affected by the COVID-19 pandemic and that this had had an impact on the Multi-Agency Risk Assessment Conference (MARAC) Operational Board. Nevertheless CJINI were of the view that, 'given the heightened concerns for victims of domestic abuse during the pandemic, it is disappointing that more focus could not have been placed on this work'.[168] However, although the PSNI chaired the MARAC Operational Board, it was recognised that they were only one organisation involved in the multi-agency arrangements, and indeed stakeholders had commended the PSNI's work in bringing together, through the Domestic Abuse Independent Advisory Group, voluntary organisations with government departments and agencies. Addressing this recommendation necessitated all agencies playing their part, and CJINI hoped that the work of the Independent Advisory Group would provide further impetus for working in partnership. CJINI thus concluded that this recommendation had been partially achieved.[169]

The third recommendation which had been made in the 2019 report had been that, 'The Police Service of Northern Ireland and the Public Prosecution Service should develop an implementation plan to further develop the prosecution team approach for cases involving domestic abuse or with a domestic motivation within three months of this report'.[170] CJINI were of the view that there had certainly been a substantial amount of activity by both the PSNI and the PPS to address this recommendation. Further enhancements had been made to the processes for the provision of evidence by the police to the PPS, and specialist prosecutors had been put in place who could develop improved working relationships with Domestic Abuse Officers in the PSNI's Public Protection Branch, in addition to supporting the work of the domestic abuse court when it is developed. However, CJINI were of the view that the action plan which had been developed could have contained more detail as to how the PSNI and the PPS would build the case using a prosecution team approach, improve the approach to dealing with victim withdrawal, ensure early consideration of evidence from body-worn video and other technology which may contain sources of evidence and ensure joint learning from complex and serious cases.[171] CJINI commented that:

> To date there has been a focus by the PSNI and the PPS on understanding in more detail the issues within the cases that need to be addressed, but now there needs to be greater detail in establishing clear plans and processes between the two organisations on addressing these issues.[172]

The Inspectors therefore encouraged the PSNI and the PPS to 'continue to develop working relationships and the prosecution team approach',[173] and concluded that this recommendation had been partially implemented.

The fourth recommendation from the 2019 report had been that:

> The Criminal Justice Board, in conjunction with its partners, should, in the nine months following the publication of this report, ensure the delivery and roll out of Northern Ireland-wide schemes to enhance the criminal justice system's approach to domestic violence and abuse, in relation to:
>
> - where volume is assessed to be sufficient, providing services to enable the clustering of domestic abuse cases to a designated court in each Administrative Court Division; and
> - a properly costed contract for an Independent Domestic Violence Advocacy service to address the safety of victims at high risk of harm.[174]

In relation to enabling the clustering of domestic abuse cases to designated courts, initial discussions had taken place with the Presiding District Judge as regards piloting a domestic violence and abuse court in Belfast. It was envisaged that this model would work in a similar manner to the arrangements in the District Judge's domestic violence court in the Magistrates' Court in Derry/Londonderry, however details had not been discussed. This work had been paused due to the ongoing pandemic. Discussions had continued regarding the proposals for an advocacy support service for victims of domestic and sexual violence and abuse in Northern Ireland, to be commissioned by the Department of Justice, and a tender had been published in December 2020.[175] However, the CJINI commented that:

> The impact of the COVID-19 pandemic on plans to establish the domestic violence court in Belfast and the length of time taken to scope out, tender for and appoint a service provider for the advocacy service clearly means that the nine-month timeframe set out in CJI's recommendation published in June 2019 has been far exceeded. Eighteen months after the publication of the inspection report CJI is disappointed that neither the domestic violence court nor the advocacy service has materialised.[176]

This recommendation was therefore assessed as not having been achieved.

It should however be noted that by October 2021 a new advocacy service, entitled 'ASSIST NI', for victims of domestic and sexual abuse had been established. A referral to this service can be made by the PSNI in circumstances where a domestic or sexual abuse crime is reported. A referral can also be made by the Rowan Sexual Assault Referral Centre, or as an action from a MARAC meeting. As the Justice Minister, Naomi Long, stated, 'ASSIST NI can provide an advocacy support service through a suite of measures, including assessing individual need, the development of safety support plans and providing impartial support and information'.[177] The three specialist organisations working in partnership to deliver the service are Belfast and Lisburn Women's Aid, Foyle Women's Aid and the Men's Advisory Project, and the service is being rolled out on a phased basis. The ASSIST NI Advocacy Service Manager, Michelle Martin, commented that:

> It is our ambition to ensure that qualifying victims of sexual and domestic violence are safe, informed and supported from the moment of reporting through the justice process. We strive to

> ensure that victims are provided with trauma-informed, victim led, bespoke support to meet individual needs and manage risk. We want to work towards a shared goal of independence, free from fear, harm and abuse creating safer lives, safer homes and safer communities.[178]

The fifth recommendation which had been made in the CJINI 2019 report was that, 'The Department of Justice should review, with input from relevant stakeholders, how potential inadequacies in current legislation regarding the act of choking or strangulation by defendants could be addressed'.[179] At the time of the follow-up inspection, the Department of Justice had established a Review framework as well as a Review Board and expert reference group. Although the Review had been delayed due to other priorities, the PPS had also undertaken work separately in this area. For example, the PPS and the PSNI had co-presented awareness raising sessions on the topic of 'attempting to choke' at the Women's Aid Conference in January 2020 and at a meeting of the South Eastern Health and Social Care Trust Domestic Violence Partnership in March 2020. Updated guidance had also been issued to prosecutors on non-fatal strangulation which emphasised the seriousness of these types of assaults.[180] CJINI therefore considered this recommendation to have been partially achieved, even though at the time of the follow-up review there was 'still a significant body of work to be completed before it could be considered achieved'.[181]

The sixth recommendation from the 2019 report had been that, 'The Department of Justice should develop plans for and consult upon legislation to introduce protection orders for stalking and harassment'.[182] Given that the Protection from Stalking legislation encompassed the introduction of Stalking Protection Orders to provide protection to those at risk of stalking, as was discussed earlier in this chapter, CJINI were thus of the view that this recommendation had been achieved.[183]

The final recommendation contained in the 2019 report had been that,

> The Public Prosecution Service for Northern Ireland, with support from criminal justice partners, should review the use of special measures in cases of domestic abuse to assess compliance with paragraph 48 of the Victim Charter[184] and take action to address any issues arising.[185]

A specific piece of work around special measures had not been undertaken to assess such compliance. CJINI did note however that section 35 of the Domestic Abuse and Civil Proceedings Act (Northern Ireland)

2021 would amend the Criminal Evidence (Northern Ireland) Order 1999 to grant automatically special measures to any victim of an offence involving domestic abuse unless they advised the court they did not wish to avail of such measures. It was thus hoped that the changes to legislation and related training delivered to prosecutors would address the issues involved. Nevertheless, CJINI could not consider the recommendation to have been achieved at the time of consideration.[186]

Domestic Abuse Protection Notices and Orders

During 2020–2021, the Department of Justice carried out further public consultations relevant to the issue of domestic abuse. For example, in December 2020 the Department launched a consultation which sought views on the creation of Domestic Abuse Protection Notices and Orders to enhance the protection available to victims.[187] Section 27 of the Domestic Abuse and Civil Proceedings Act (Northern Ireland) 2021 states that the Department may, by regulations, make provision to bring forward steps or measures to protect victims of domestic abuse, including through such Notices and Orders. In the December 2020 consultation it was proposed that a civil Domestic Abuse Protection Notice, which would be issued by the police, would provide immediate protection from all forms of domestic abuse. It was proposed that such a Notice could be utilised where a senior police officer had reasonable grounds for believing that a person had been abusive to someone to whom they were personally connected and that the Notice was necessary in order to provide protection from domestic abuse or a risk of domestic abuse. For such a Notice to be issued, the victim would have to be aged 16 or over and the alleged perpetrator aged 18 or over. A Domestic Abuse Protection Notice could require the alleged perpetrator to refrain from contacting the victim or coming within a certain distance of their home, or require them to leave the victim's home. It was proposed that a Domestic Abuse Protection Notice could last for up to four or seven days, at which point an application would have to be made to the Magistrates' Court for a civil Domestic Abuse Protection Order. Such an Order would provide a flexible and longer-term protection. It was proposed that an Order could last from approximately six months to one or two years, but could be longer in certain circumstances. Orders would be available in both civil and criminal courts. An application for an Order could be made by the victim, by the police, or potentially by specified third parties. Also, any other person would be able to apply with the leave of the family court. In addition, Orders could be made by the criminal, civil or family court, of its own volition, during other court proceedings. It was proposed that Orders could in the longer term also include provisions such as requiring an individual to be subject to electronic monitoring or to attend a behavioural change programme. Breach of an Order would be a criminal offence, with a maximum penalty of up to five years' imprisonment, or a fine, or both. A breach could also be dealt with as a civil contempt of court at the request of the victim.[188]

A summary of responses to the consultation was published in May 2021.[189] The majority of responses were supportive of the proposal to introduce such Notices and Orders. However, the Department of Justice agreed to undertake a number of actions before commencing work on the drafting of regulations and guidance. For example, the Department would conduct a human rights impact assessment, including in relation to the time period for making a Domestic Abuse Protection Order and any future electronic monitoring; and engage with the Judicial Studies Board as regards raising awareness of such Notices and Orders amongst the judiciary.[190]

On 22 March 2022, the Justice Minister reported to the Northern Ireland Assembly that the commencement of section 27 of the Domestic Abuse and Civil Proceedings Act (Northern Ireland) 2021 in February 2022 meant that regulations could be brought forward to provide for Domestic Abuse Protection Notices and Orders. This was now a priority work area for the Department of Justice. Preparatory work had begun on considering the framework for the draft regulations and a guidance document for practitioners, which would explain the process for the Notices and Orders and how they will work in practice. Officials from the Department of Justice had joined a working group led by the Home Office and the Ministry of Justice to learn from their experiences in order to inform policy development and operational preparations.[191]

Conclusion

The period of time spanned by this chapter has undoubtedly been dominated by the COVID-19 pandemic. The public health emergency was an unprecedented situation which caused intractable difficulties for Northern Ireland, as it did for all other jurisdictions globally. Until the COVID-19 vaccines were widely rolled out in Northern Ireland, the most effective way of preventing the spread of the virus was to keep people apart to as great an extent as was possible, which was of course the premise behind the lockdown measures which were implemented. However, such measures also had the effect of increasing the suffering of many victims of domestic abuse. At the international level, human rights entities urged governments to adopt measures to address the rise in levels of domestic abuse in the context of the pandemic, and meritorious steps were taken in Northern Ireland. In particular, the PSNI developed its collaborative work with other agencies in order to provide a proactive and effective response.

There were also other very meritorious steps taken during 2020–2022 towards improving responses to domestic abuse in Northern Ireland, and it is clear that this is now very much a priority of the Department of Justice. The introduction of domestic homicide reviews is to be welcomed, and it is to be hoped that such reviews will contribute towards the prevention of future domestic homicides and the improvement of service responses for victims of domestic abuse. In addition, an advocacy service, entitled 'ASSIST NI' has been established for victims of domestic and sexual abuse. Likewise, work is ongoing in relation to Domestic Abuse Protection Notices and Orders.

Prior to 2021, the legislative response to domestic abuse in Northern Ireland was substantially 'lagging behind' those of the other jurisdictions in the UK and Ireland. However, the passing of the Domestic Abuse and Civil Proceedings Act (Northern Ireland) 2021 constituted a crucial development in the response of the criminal justice system in Northern Ireland to domestic abuse. The enactment of this legislation essentially served to ameliorate a clear deficiency and, by criminalising coercive control, brought Northern Ireland's legislative response to this issue into line with human rights standards. Additionally, the Protection from Stalking Act (Northern Ireland) 2022 allowed Northern Ireland to 'catch up' with the other jurisdictions in the UK in its legislative response to stalking; and the introduction of an offence of non-fatal strangulation or asphyxiation under section 28 of the Justice (Sexual Offences and Trafficking Victims Act (Northern Ireland) 2022 is also meritorious.

However, legislation alone is not sufficient to address the issue of domestic abuse. An effective criminal justice response is also heavily dependent upon how such legislation is then used by the relevant agencies within the criminal justice system, such as the police, prosecutors and the courts. As CJINI's follow-up report of 2021 demonstrates, although very valuable work has been carried out as regards improving criminal justice responses to domestic abuse in Northern Ireland, there is more that still needs to be done. In addition, it is important to remember that although ensuring an effective criminal justice response is vital to addressing the issue of domestic abuse, it is essential that this forms part of a holistic approach, as will be discussed in Chapter 5.

Notes

1 'New Decade, New Approach', January 2020, https://assets.publishing.service.gov.uk/government/uploads/system/uploads/attachment_data/file/856998/2020-01-08_a_new_decade__a_new_approach.pdf
2 BBC News, 'Coronavirus: Strict New Curbs on Life in UK Announced by PM', 24 March 2020, www.bbc.co.uk/news/uk-52012432. See Cabinet Office, 'Guidance: Staying at Home and Away from Others (Social Distancing)', updated 1 May 2020, www.gov.uk/government/publications/full-guidance-on-staying-at-home-and-away-from-others/full-guidance-on-staying-at-home-and-away-from-others
3 BBC News, op. cit.
4 Department of Health, 'COVID-19 Statistics Northern Ireland', 31 December 2021, app.powerbi.com/view?r=eyJrIjoiODJjOGE3ZDUtM2ViNy00YjBlLTllMjktOTNjZjlkODJhODU4IiwidCI6ImU3YTEzYWVhLTk0MzctNGRiNy1hMjJiLWNmYWE0Y2UzM2I2ZSJ9
5 World Health Organization, 'COVID-19 and Violence against Women. What the Health Sector/System Can Do', 7 April 2020, apps.who.int/iris/bitstream/handle/10665/331699/WHO-SRH-20.04-eng.pdf?ua=1. For further discussion of domestic abuse as a health issue, see Nakray K. (ed.), *Gender-based Violence and Public Health*, 2013, Routledge, Abingdon.
6 UN Committee on Economic, Social and Cultural Rights, General Comment No. 14: The Right to the Highest Attainable Standard of Health (Art. 12), (2000), para. 21.
7 Para. 51.
8 UN Committee on the Elimination of Discrimination against Women, General Recommendation No. 24: Article 12 of the Convention (women and health) (1999), para. 13.
9 Para. 15.
10 Para. 15.
11 General Assembly Resolution 45/114 (1990), para. 1. For further discussion of the approach of the UN human rights bodies to domestic violence as a health issue, see McQuigg R.J.A., 'Gender Based Violence and the Legal Perspective: An International Overview', in K. Nakray (ed.), *Gender-based Violence and Public Health*, 2013, Routledge, Abingdon, 40–53.
12 Doyle J.L. and McWilliams M., 'Intimate Partner Violence in Conflict and Post-Conflict Societies', May 2018, Political Settlements Research Programme, Edinburgh, at 4.
13 Women's Aid NI, 'Women's Aid NI Statement on Covid-19 and the Domestic Abuse Sector', 20 March 2020, www.womensaidni.org/womens-aid-ni-statement-on-covid-19-and-the-domestic-abuse-sector/
14 Northern Ireland Statistics and Research Agency, 'Domestic Abuse Incidents and Crimes Recorded by the Police in Northern Ireland: Update to 31 December 2020', 25 February 2021.
15 Amnesty International UK, 'Northern Ireland: With Domestic Violence at All-time High, Funding Urgently Needed for Frontline Groups', 18 May

2020, www.amnesty.org.uk/press-releases/northern-ireland-domestic-viole nce-all-time-high-funding-urgently-needed-frontline

16 BBC News, 'Coronavirus: Three Domestic Killings since Lockdown Began', 28 April 2020, www.bbc.co.uk/news/uk-northern-ireland-52440662

17 Women's Aid, 'Covid-19: One Year On', 23 March 2021, www.womensai dni.org/covid-19-one-year-on/

18 UN Special Rapporteur on violence against women, its causes and consequences, 'States Must Combat Domestic Violence in the Context of Covid-19 Lockdowns', 27 March 2020, www.ohchr.org/EN/NewsEvents/Pages/DisplayNews.aspx?NewsID=25749&LangID=E

19 Para. 3.

20 Department of Justice and Department of Health, 'Coronavirus (Covid-19) – Support for Victims of Domestic Abuse', www.health-ni.gov.uk/sites/default/files/publications/health/Covid-19-Support-for-VofDA.pdf

21 Department of Justice and Department of Health, op. cit., at 2–3.

22 Northern Ireland Policing Board, 'Report on the Thematic Review of the Policing Response to COVID-19', 2020, www.nipolicingboard.org.uk/sites/nipb/files/publications/report-on-the-thematic-review-of-the-policing-responser-to-covid-19.PDF, at 95.

23 Northern Ireland Policing Board, op. cit., at 94.

24 Department of Justice and Department of Health, op. cit., at 4.

25 Northern Ireland Policing Board, op. cit., at 93–94.

26 Northern Ireland Policing Board, op. cit., at 94.

27 Northern Ireland Policing Board, op. cit., at 95.

28 Northern Ireland Policing Board, op. cit., at 94–95.

29 Northern Ireland Policing Board, op. cit., at 104.

30 UK Government, 'Pharmacies Launch Codeword Scheme to Offer "Lifeline" to Domestic Abuse Victims', 14 January 2021, www.gov.uk/gov ernment/news/pharmacies-launch-codeword-scheme-to-offer-lifeline-to-domestic-abuse-victims

31 UK Government, op. cit.

32 UK Government, op. cit.

33 Department of Justice, 'Domestic Homicide Reviews – Consultation', July 2018, www.justice-ni.gov.uk/sites/default/files/consultations/justice/dhr-consultation.pdf

34 Department of Justice, 'Domestic Homicide Reviews – A Consultation. Summary of Responses and Way Forward', January 2019, www.justice-ni.gov.uk/sites/default/files/consultations/justice/dhr-summary-of-responses.pdf

35 Department of Justice, 'Long Introduces Domestic Homicide Reviews and Appoints Panel Chairs', 10 December 2020, www.justice-ni.gov.uk/news/long-introduces-domestic-homicide-reviews-and-appoints-panel-chairs

36 Department of Justice (2020), op. cit.

37 Department of Justice (2020), op. cit.

38 Domestic Abuse and Family Proceedings Bill, Explanatory and Financial Memorandum, at 1–2.

39 BBC News, 'New Abuse Law "Held Up by Lack of NI Assembly"', 19 January 2018, www.bbc.co.uk/news/uk-northern-ireland-42739589
40 Northern Ireland Assembly, 'Official Report: Tuesday 28 April 2020', Naomi Long MLA, Justice Minister.
41 Discussion of this Act can also be found in McQuigg R.J.A., 'Northern Ireland's new offence of domestic abuse' (2021) *Statute Law Review*, early online access: https://doi.org/10.1093/slr/hmab013
42 Northern Ireland Assembly, 'Official Report: Tuesday 28 April 2020', Naomi Long MLA, Justice Minister.
43 Northern Ireland Assembly, 'Official Report: Tuesday 28 April 2020', Naomi Long MLA, Justice Minister.
44 Northern Ireland Assembly, 'Official Report: Tuesday 28 April 2020', Paul Givan MLA.
45 Northern Ireland Assembly, 'Official Report: Tuesday 28 April 2020', Kellie Armstrong MLA.
46 Domestic Abuse and Family Proceedings Bill, Explanatory and Financial Memorandum, at 4.
47 Domestic Abuse and Family Proceedings Bill, Explanatory and Financial Memorandum, at 5.
48 Domestic Abuse and Family Proceedings Bill, Explanatory and Financial Memorandum, at 6.
49 Domestic Abuse and Family Proceedings Bill, Explanatory and Financial Memorandum, at 7.
50 Serious Crime Act 2015, section 76(1)(c).
51 Section 76(1)(d).
52 Section 76(4)(a).
53 Section 76(4)(b).
54 Domestic Abuse Act 2018, section 39(1)(b).
55 Section 39(1)(c).
56 Section 39(2)(a).
57 Section 39(2)(b).
58 Northern Ireland Assembly, 'Official Report: Tuesday 28 April 2020', Naomi Long MLA, Justice Minister.
59 Herring J., *Domestic Abuse and Human Rights*, 2020, Intersentia, Cambridge, at 124.
60 Bishop C. and Bettinson V., 'Evidencing domestic violence, including behaviour that falls under the new offence of "coercive and controlling behaviour"', (2018) 22 *International Journal of Evidence and Proof* 3 at 10–12.
61 Domestic Abuse and Family Proceedings Bill, Explanatory and Financial Memorandum, at 7.
62 Northern Ireland Assembly, 'Official Report: Tuesday 28 April 2020', Naomi Long MLA, Justice Minister.
63 Domestic Abuse and Civil Proceedings Act (Northern Ireland) 2021, section 3(1).
64 Section 3(2).

65 Domestic Abuse and Family Proceedings Bill, Explanatory and Financial Memorandum, at 8.
66 Domestic Abuse and Family Proceedings Bill, Explanatory and Financial Memorandum, at 8.
67 Domestic Abuse and Family Proceedings Bill, Explanatory and Financial Memorandum, at 8.
68 Domestic Abuse and Civil Proceedings Act (Northern Ireland) 2021, section 5(2)(a).
69 Section 5(2)(b).
70 Section 5(2)(c).
71 Section 5(2)(d).
72 Section 5(2)(e).
73 Northern Ireland Assembly, Official Report: 28 April 2020.
74 Domestic Violence Act 2018, section 39(1).
75 Section 39(4).
76 Cairns I., 'What counts as "domestic"? Family relationships and the proposed criminalization of domestic abuse in Scotland', (2017) 21 *Edinburgh Law Review* 262 at 265–266.
77 Domestic Abuse and Family Proceedings Bill, Explanatory and Financial Memorandum, at 2.
78 Cairns, op. cit., at 265. See also Connelly C. and Cavanagh K., 'Domestic abuse, civil protection orders and the "new criminologies": Is there any value in engaging with the law', (2007) 15 *Feminist Legal Studies* 259 at 279; and Humphreys C. and Thiara R.K., 'Neither justice nor protection: Women's experiences of post-separation violence', (2003) 25 *Journal of Social Welfare and Family Law* 195.
79 Cairns, op. cit., at 265. See also Barnett A., '"Like gold dust these days": Domestic violence fact-finding hearings in child contact cases', (2015) 23 *Feminist Legal Studies* 47.
80 Mills O., 'Effects of domestic violence on children', (2008) *Family Law* 165.
81 Northern Ireland Assembly, 'Official Report: Tuesday 28 April 2020', Naomi Long MLA, Justice Minister.
82 Domestic Abuse and Civil Proceedings Act (Northern Ireland) 2021, section 9(3)(a).
83 Section 9(3)(b).
84 Committee for Justice, Report on the Domestic Abuse and Family Proceedings Bill, Report: NIA 48/17-22, 15 October 2020, at para. 26.
85 Home Office, 'Controlling or Coercive Behaviour in an Intimate or Family Relationship: Statutory Guidance Framework', December 2015, at 6.
86 Department of Justice, 'Abusive Behaviour in an Intimate or Family Relationship – Domestic Abuse Offence, Statutory Guidance, Part 1 of the Domestic Abuse and Civil Proceedings Act (Northern Ireland) 2021 and Other Matters as to Criminal Law or Procedure Relating to Domestic Abuse in Northern Ireland', February 2022, at 20.
87 Committee for Justice, op. cit., at para. 376.
88 Committee for Justice, op. cit., at para. 378.

89 Department of Justice (2022), op. cit., at 17.
90 Department of Justice (2022), op. cit., at 17.
91 Serious Crime Act 2015, section 76(8)(b).
92 Section 76(8)(a).
93 Section 76(10).
94 Domestic Abuse and Civil Proceedings Act (Northern Ireland) 2021, section 14(a).
95 Section 14(b).
96 Serious Crime Act 2015, section 76(11)(a); and Domestic Violence Act, section 39(3)(b).
97 Bishop C., 'Domestic Violence: The Limitations of a Legal Response' in S. Hilder and V. Bettinson (eds.), *Domestic Violence – Interdisciplinary Perspectives on Protection, Prevention and Intervention*, 2016, Palgrave Macmillan, 59–79 at 72.
98 Bishop, op. cit., at 72.
99 Domestic Abuse and Family Proceedings Bill, Explanatory and Financial Memorandum, at 2.
100 Northern Ireland Assembly, 'Official Report: Tuesday 28 April 2020', Naomi Long MLA, Justice Minister.
101 Domestic Abuse and Family Proceedings Bill, Explanatory and Financial Memorandum, at 11.
102 Committee for Justice, op. cit., at para. 420.
103 Bettinson V. and Robson J., 'Prosecuting coercive control: Reforming storytelling in the courtroom', (2020) 12 *Criminal Law Review* 1107 at 1110.
104 Bettinson and Robson, op. cit., at 1108.
105 Bishop and Bettinson, op. cit., at 6. See further, Ellison L., 'Prosecuting domestic violence without victim participation', (2002) 65 *Modern Law Review* 834; Robinson A. and Cook D., 'Understanding victim retraction in cases of domestic violence: Specialist courts, government policy, and victim-centred justice', (2006) 9 *Contemporary Justice Review* 189; and Cretney A. and Davis G., 'Prosecuting domestic assault: Victims failing courts, or courts failing victims?', (1997) 36 *Howard Journal* 146.
106 Bettinson and Robson, op. cit., at 1114.
107 Bettinson and Robson, op. cit., at 1114.
108 Department of Justice (2022), op. cit., at 22.
109 Department of Justice (2022), op. cit., at 22.
110 Department of Justice (2022), op. cit., at 22.
111 Department of Justice (2022), op. cit., at 24–26.
112 Criminal Evidence (Northern Ireland) Order 1999, article 11.
113 Article 12.
114 Article 13.
115 Article 15.
116 Article 16.
117 Northern Ireland Assembly, 'Official Report: Tuesday 28 April 2020', Naomi Long MLA, Justice Minister.

118 Northern Ireland Assembly, 'Official Report: Tuesday 28 April 2020', Paul Givan MLA.
119 Northern Ireland Assembly, 'Official Report: Tuesday 28 April 2020', Naomi Long MLA, Justice Minister.
120 Domestic Abuse and Civil Proceedings Act (Northern Ireland) 2021, section 16(2)(a).
121 Section 16(2)(b).
122 Section 16(2)(c).
123 Section 18(2)(a).
124 Section 18(2)(b).
125 Section 18(2)(c).
126 Section 18(2)(d).
127 Section 18(2)(e).
128 Section 18(3)(a).
129 Domestic Abuse and Family Proceedings Bill, Explanatory and Financial Memorandum, at 12.
130 Domestic Abuse and Civil Proceedings Act (Northern Ireland) 2021, section 16(3)(b).
131 Committee for Justice, op. cit., at para. 70.
132 Department of Justice (2022), op. cit., at para. 4.6.
133 United Nations Centre for Social Development and Humanitarian Affairs, Strategies for Confronting Domestic Violence: A Resource Manual 7 (1993) U.N.Doc.ST/CSDHA/20 (1993) at 38, as quoted by Thomas C., 'Domestic Violence', in K.D. Askin and D.M. Koenig (eds.), *Women and International Human Rights Law* (Vol.1), 1999, Transnational Publishers Inc., New York, 219–256 at 227.
134 The main role of the Sentencing Council is to issue guidelines on sentencing, which must be followed by the courts unless it is in the interests of justice not to do so.
135 Sentencing Council, 'Overarching Principles: Domestic Abuse', effective from 24 May 2018, www.sentencingcouncil.org.uk/overarching-guides/crown-court/item/domestic-abuse/
136 Abusive Behaviour and Sexual Harm (Scotland) Act 2016, section 1(2)(a).
137 Section 1(2)(b).
138 Section 1(5).
139 Domestic Violence Act 2018, section 40(5).
140 Domestic Abuse and Civil Proceedings Act (Northern Ireland) 2021 (Commencement No. 1) Order (Northern Ireland 2022.
141 Crown Prosecution Service, 'Stalking Analysis Reveals Domestic Abuse Link', 4 December 2020, www.cps.gov.uk/cps/news/stalking-analysis-reveals-domestic-abuse-link
142 Criminal Justice and Licensing (Scotland) Act 2010, section 39.
143 The Protection from Harassment Act 1997 was amended by the Protection of Freedoms Act 2012 to include an offence of stalking under section 2A and an offence of stalking involving fear of violence or serious alarm or distress under section 4A.

144 Department of Justice (2019), op. cit., at 5.
145 Department of Justice (2019), op. cit., at 21.
146 Protection from Stalking Act (Northern Ireland) 2022, section 7(2). See also Protection from Stalking Bill, Explanatory and Financial Memorandum, at 6.
147 Section 7(2).
148 Department of Justice, 'Long Welcomes New Stalking Legislation', 22 February 2022, www.justice-ni.gov.uk/news/long-welcomes-new-stalking-legislation#:~:text=The%20legislation%20creates%20a%20new,particular%20risks%20associated%20with%20stalking
149 Department of Justice, 'Non-Fatal Strangulation: A Public Consultation', July 2021, www.justice-ni.gov.uk/consultations/consultation-non-fatal-strangulation. For discussion of strangulations and domestic abuse, see Douglas H. and Fitzgerald R., 'Strangulation, domestic violence and the legal response', (2014) 26 *Sydney Law Review* 231; and Edwards S., 'The strangulation of female partners', (2015) 12 *Criminal Law Review* 949.
150 Criminal Justice Inspection Northern Ireland, 'No Excuse: A Thematic Inspection of the Handling of Domestic Violence and Abuse Cases by the Criminal Justice System in Northern Ireland. A Follow-Up Review of the Inspection Recommendations', April 2021, www.cjini.org/getattachment/48e855ca-cd40-4283-83c2-720cf49b5c94/report.aspx, at 31.
151 Department of Justice (2021), op. cit., at paras. 25–27.
152 Serious Crime Act 2015, section 75A(3).
153 Section 75A(2).
154 Section 75A(6).
155 Section 75A(5).
156 Department of Justice, 'Non-Fatal Strangulation – Summary of Consultation Responses and Way Forward', November 2021, www.justice-ni.gov.uk/sites/default/files/publications/justice/annex-a-non-fatal-strangulation-summary-way-forward.pdf
157 Justice (Sexual Offences and Trafficking Victims) Act (Northern Ireland) 2022, section 28(1).
158 Section 28(2).
159 Section 28(3).
160 Section 28(6).
161 Section 28(11).
162 Section 28(10).
163 Criminal Justice Inspection Northern Ireland, op. cit.
164 Criminal Justice Inspection Northern Ireland, 'No Excuse: A Thematic Inspection of the Handling of Domestic Violence and Abuse Cases by the Criminal Justice System in Northern Ireland', June 2019, www.cjini.org/getattachment/079beabb-d094-40e9-8738-0f84cd347ae8/report.aspx, at 12.
165 Criminal Justice Inspection Northern Ireland (2021), op. cit., at 14–18.
166 Criminal Justice Inspection Northern Ireland (2021), op. cit., at 14–18.
167 Criminal Justice Inspection Northern Ireland (2019), op. cit., at 12.
168 Criminal Justice Inspection Northern Ireland (2021), op. cit., at 20.

169 Criminal Justice Inspection Northern Ireland (2021), op. cit., at 18–20.
170 Criminal Justice Inspection Northern Ireland (2019), op. cit., at 12.
171 Criminal Justice Inspection Northern Ireland (2021), op. cit., at 20–25.
172 Criminal Justice Inspection Northern Ireland (2021), op. cit., at 24.
173 Criminal Justice Inspection Northern Ireland (2021), op. cit., at 25.
174 Criminal Justice Inspection Northern Ireland (2019), op. cit., at 12.
175 Criminal Justice Inspection Northern Ireland (2021), op. cit., at 25–29.
176 Criminal Justice Inspection Northern Ireland (2021), op. cit., at 29.
177 Department of Justice, 'Long Welcomes Advocacy Service for Sexual and Domestic Abuse Victims', 4 October 2021, www.justice-ni.gov.uk/news/long-welcomes-advocacy-service-sexual-and-domestic-abuse-victims
178 Department of Justice, 'Long Welcomes Advocacy Service for Sexual and Domestic Abuse Victims' (2021), op. cit.
179 Criminal Justice Inspection Northern Ireland (2019), op. cit., at 13.
180 Criminal Justice Inspection Northern Ireland (2021), op. cit., at 29–31.
181 Criminal Justice Inspection Northern Ireland (2021), op. cit., at 31.
182 Criminal Justice Inspection Northern Ireland (2019), op. cit., at 13.
183 Criminal Justice Inspection Northern Ireland (2021), op. cit., at 31–32.
184 Department of Justice, 'Victim Charter – A Charter for Victims of Crime', September 2015, www.justice-ni.gov.uk/sites/default/files/publications/doj/victim-charter.pdf. Paragraph 48 states that a victim may be regarded as being 'intimidated' when giving evidence if they have experienced domestic violence.
185 Criminal Justice Inspection Northern Ireland (2019), op. cit., at 13.
186 Criminal Justice Inspection Northern Ireland (2021), op. cit., at 32–34.
187 Department of Justice, 'Enhancing Legal Protections for Victims of Domestic Abuse – A Public Consultation', December 2020, www.justice-ni.gov.uk/sites/default/files/consultations/justice/consultation-paper-on-dapns-and-dapos-dec.pdf
188 Department of Justice, 'Enhancing Legal Protections for Victims of Domestic Abuse – A Public Consultation' (2020), op. cit., at 33–34.
189 Department of Justice, 'Enhancing Legal Protections for Victims of Domestic Abuse – A Consultation. Summary of Responses', May 2021, www.justice-ni.gov.uk/sites/default/files/publications/justice/enhancing-legal-protections-for-victims-summary-way-forward.pdf
190 Department of Justice 'Enhancing Legal Protections for Victims of Domestic Abuse – A Consultation. Summary of Responses' (2021), op. cit., at 71–72.
191 Northern Ireland Assembly, 'Official Report: Tuesday 22 March 2022', Naomi Long MLA, Justice Minister.

5 Conclusions

The aim of this chapter is to summarise the key points and conclusions from the preceding discussion. In addition, the chapter emphasises that although the criminal justice system plays an essential role in addressing domestic abuse, it is important to remember that providing an effective response to this issue requires a holistic approach involving other aspects such as the provision of sufficient social support measures for victims.

Summary

Northern Ireland is undoubtedly a jurisdiction with a troubled past. For this reason, studies of violence relating to Northern Ireland have largely focused on the political violence which indisputably constitutes an important part of the history of this jurisdiction. However, many people in Northern Ireland have experienced and are indeed still suffering from violence within their own homes. This book has aimed to provide a detailed study of criminal justice responses to domestic abuse in this jurisdiction.

The criminal justice system clearly plays a vital role in responding to domestic abuse. As was discussed in Chapter 2, there is much discussion in the academic literature of the elements which are needed in order to provide an effective criminal justice response to this issue. Not only must adequate legislation be put in place, but key agencies within the criminal justice system, such as the police, the prosecution service and the courts, must also respond in an effective manner. In addition, human rights entities at both the UN and regional levels have considered in some detail the standards which should be applied in this area.

Chapter 3 analysed the responses of the criminal justice system in Northern Ireland to domestic abuse prior to 2020. Political violence was a part of life in Northern Ireland for around 30 years from the late 1960s until the late 1990s, and the 'Troubles' impacted greatly

DOI: 10.4324/9781003261650-5

upon the response of the criminal justice system to domestic abuse. During this time, this issue received very little attention from the criminal justice system, with resources being focused instead on addressing the ongoing political violence. However, the focus of the chapter was on analysing much more recent developments, specifically during the decade from around 2010 until 2019. By the end of 2019 the response of the criminal justice system in Northern Ireland to domestic abuse had improved greatly, and initiatives such as the Domestic Violence and Abuse Disclosure Scheme were certainly important steps in this process. In addition, in March 2016, the Department of Health, Social Services and Public Safety and the Department of Justice issued their seven-year strategy on 'Stopping Domestic and Sexual Violence and Abuse in Northern Ireland'.[1] The Department of Justice also launched public consultations in 2018 on a proposed model for the introduction of domestic homicide reviews in Northern Ireland,[2] and on the creation of a new offence of stalking.[3]

Nevertheless, difficulties remained, particularly in relation to the lack of legislation criminalising coercive control. Although in 2016 the Department of Justice had launched a public consultation on domestic abuse which included the question of whether a specific offence capturing coercive and controlling behaviour should be enacted,[4] a proposition which received overwhelming support from respondents,[5] progress on this aspect stalled due to the collapse of the Assembly in January 2017.

Chapter 4 analysed criminal justice responses to domestic abuse in Northern Ireland during 2020–2022. Developments during this time period were clearly influenced substantially by the COVID-19 pandemic which engulfed the world from early 2020. The associated lockdown measures which were adopted by many States globally served to create conditions which contributed to significant increases in levels of domestic abuse internationally. Human rights entities urged governments to adopt measures to address the rise in rates of domestic abuse in the context of the pandemic, and meritorious steps were taken in Northern Ireland. In particular, the PSNI developed its collaborative work with other agencies in order to provide a proactive and effective response.

It is clear that addressing the issue of domestic abuse is now very much a priority of the Department of Justice. For example, the introduction in December 2020 of domestic homicide reviews was a very welcome development which should serve to contribute towards the prevention of future domestic homicides and the improvement of service responses for victims of domestic abuse. In particular, the passing of the Domestic Abuse and Civil Proceedings Act (Northern Ireland) 2021 constituted a crucial development in the response of the criminal justice system in Northern Ireland to domestic abuse. By criminalising coercive control, this legislation served to ameliorate a clear deficiency in the legislative response of this jurisdiction, and brought Northern Ireland into line with human rights standards in this regard. Also, the Protection from Stalking Act (Northern Ireland) 2022 allowed Northern Ireland to 'catch up' with the other jurisdictions in the UK in its legislative response to stalking.

However, as the follow-up report of April 2021 by Criminal Justice Inspection Northern Ireland (CJINI) demonstrates,[6] although very valuable work has been carried out as regards improving criminal justice responses to domestic abuse in Northern Ireland, there is more that still needs to be done. Nevertheless, it is worth noting that since the publication of this report, further steps have been taken to implement the recommendations of CJINI. For example, by October 2021 a new advocacy service, entitled 'ASSIST NI', for victims of domestic and sexual abuse had been established; and an offence of non-fatal strangulation or asphyxiation was enacted in April 2022 under section 28 of the Justice (Sexual Offences and Trafficking Victims) Act (Northern Ireland) 2022.

It must be remembered though that whilst ensuring an effective criminal justice response is crucial to addressing the issue of domestic abuse, it is vital that this forms part of a holistic approach.

The Need for a Holistic Approach to Addressing Domestic Abuse

It has been accepted by many commentators that criminal justice responses to domestic abuse are inadequate in themselves.[7] Whilst it is undoubtedly essential to ensure that appropriate legislation is in place, and that the relevant agencies within the criminal justice system are acting in an effective manner, there are other aspects of responding to domestic abuse which are of equal importance, such as the provision of social support measures for victims and increasing awareness within society as a whole.[8] As Schneider states, 'Legal intervention may provide women certain protection from battering, but it does not provide women housing, support, child care, employment, community acceptance, or love. It also does not deal with the economic realities of life'.[9] Randall argues that legal responses can only be part of a comprehensive strategy to deal with such a complex problem as domestic abuse.[10] Schneider comments that far more important than criminalisation,

> is the need for provision of state and state-supported resources to deal with the real problems that battered women face – child care, shelters, welfare, work… – and thus make it possible for women to have the economic and social independence that is a prerequisite to women's freedom from abuse.[11]

Whilst there have certainly been a number of very meritorious responses to the issue of domestic abuse in Northern Ireland, problems nevertheless remain. A full discussion of responses other than those relating to the criminal justice system is beyond the scope of this book. However, in a joint statement of March 2021 from a number of bodies working in the area of combating domestic abuse, including Women's Aid NI, it was asserted that there was still serious concern regarding,

> the lack of meaningful partnership working between the UK government, devolved administrations in Wales, Scotland and Northern Ireland, and our specialist sector. This has limited the ability of all nations and regions to meet the needs of women and girls and the life-saving specialist services that support them.[12]

Essentially, 'urgent action' was needed on 'funding, equal protection and support, prevention and practical measures to protect women and girls experiencing violence and abuse during COVID 19'. The statement asserted that, 'Whilst the UK government has delivered emergency funding for the VAWG sector over the past year, it has been piecemeal, fragmented and unequal'. In particular, 'Specialist services in Northern Ireland did not receive comparable levels of funding to other nations'. Likewise, research carried out in December 2021 highlighted the 'lack of any additional or targeted funding for the (domestic abuse) sector in Northern Ireland' during the pandemic.[13]

The joint statement noted that although the 'Ask for ANI' scheme (which was discussed in Chapter 4) 'was born from the urgent need to improve gateways to help for women trapped at home with their abuser', it was not launched until nearly a year after the onset of the pandemic, and there had been 'continued concerns with how this is working across all four nations in the UK, the level of training for pharmacy staff responding to disclosures, as well as how effectively such schemes link up to local specialist support services'. The statement concluded that:

> violence against women is still not factored in at the highest levels of the pandemic response, not seen as a fundamental priority in the public health response we need. As the first year of COVID 19

> comes to end, we cannot return to 'business as usual'. We need a new approach, which equally protects all women and girls, and ends the societal inequalities that drive violence and abuse against them.

In addition, it is of particular note that Northern Ireland is currently the only jurisdiction within the UK which does not have a strategy specifically dedicated to addressing gender-based violence. However, on 9 March 2021, Women's Aid launched a petition calling on the Northern Ireland Assembly to develop and implement a strategy on violence against women and girls. As noted by Women's Aid, 'To effectively tackle violence against women, coordinated action from government is required, including preventative measures, early intervention and protection, and victim-centred justice to address the lack of services and barriers faced by women and girls'.[14] On 10 January 2022, the Northern Ireland Executive Office, the Department of Justice and the Department of Health together published a 'Call for Views' to inform the development of a 'Domestic and Sexual Abuse Strategy' to be led by the Department of Justice and the Department of Health, and an 'Equally Safe Strategy: a Strategy to Tackle Violence Against Women and Girls' to be led by the Executive Office. Those with lived experience, frontline services, researchers, academics and the general public were invited to submit by 21 March 2022 views on issues that could assist in informing the content and direction of these two new strategies. It is intended that the 'Domestic and Sexual Abuse Strategy' will have a very specific focus on these types of abuse, whilst the 'Equally Safe Strategy' will have a broader scope and will encompass 'other acts and threats of gender based violence that result in, or may result in physical, sexual or psychological harm or suffering to women, whether occurring in public or in private life, in the physical world or online'.[15]

Conclusion

In conclusion therefore, criminal justice responses to domestic abuse in Northern Ireland have certainly developed immensely during a relatively short period of time. By contrast to the dark days of the 'Troubles' during which domestic abuse was largely ignored, due to the all-encompassing priority of addressing the political violence which engulfed Northern Ireland for around 30 years, addressing domestic abuse is now a key priority of the Department of Justice. It is true that responses to domestic abuse in Northern Ireland have tended to 'lag behind' those of other parts of the UK, however this is perhaps unsurprising, given that this jurisdiction has endured such a troubled past. The criminalisation of coercive and controlling behaviour with the passing of the Domestic Abuse and Civil Proceedings Act (Northern Ireland) 2021 constitutes a particular milestone in criminal justice responses to domestic abuse in this jurisdiction.

At the time of writing, COVID-19 remains an ongoing concern in Northern Ireland, as it does around the globe, however further lockdown measures with the attendant risks for victims of domestic abuse seem unlikely. Although further steps remain necessary, immense progress has been made in improving criminal justice responses to domestic abuse in this jurisdiction. It must of course be remembered that the criminal justice system does not operate in a vacuum and, as with any issue, criminal justice responses to domestic abuse are not in themselves sufficient. The additional pressures on domestic abuse service provision which have accompanied the COVID-19 pandemic have served to emphasise the need for sufficient levels of funding to be afforded to such services. Media coverage of the increased risks to victims of domestic abuse in situations of lockdown has raised awareness of the need for effective responses to domestic abuse. The challenge must now be for Northern Ireland to continue to improve its response to domestic abuse, both as regards the criminal justice system and beyond.

Notes

1 Department of Health, Social Services and Public Safety and Department of Justice, 'Stopping Domestic and Sexual Violence and Abuse in Northern Ireland – A Seven Year Strategy', March 2016, www.justice-ni.gov.uk/sites/default/files/publications/doj/stopping-domestic-sexual-violence-ni.pdf
2 Department of Justice, 'Domestic Homicide Reviews – Consultation', July 2018, www.justice-ni.gov.uk/sites/default/files/consultations/justice/dhr-consultation.pdf
3 Department of Justice, 'Stalking – A Serious Concern. A Consultation on the Creation of a New Offence of Stalking in Northern Ireland. Consultation Report and Summary of Responses', 1 November 2019, www.justice-ni.gov.uk/sites/default/files/publications/justice/stalking-consultation-report-responses.pdf, 3–4.
4 Department of Justice, 'Domestic Abuse Offence and Domestic Violence Disclosure Scheme – A Consultation', 5 February 2016, www.justice-ni.gov.uk/sites/default/files/consultations/doj/consultation-domestic-violence.PDF
5 Department of Justice, 'Domestic Abuse Offence and Domestic Violence Disclosure Scheme – A Consultation, Summary of Responses', 2016, www.justice-ni.gov.uk/sites/default/files/consultations/justice/domestic-abuse-offence-domestic-violence-disclosure-scheme-summary-of-responses.pdf, para. 1.9.

6 Criminal Justice Inspection Northern Ireland, 'No Excuse: A Thematic Inspection of the Handling of Domestic Violence and Abuse Cases by the Criminal Justice System in Northern Ireland. A Follow-Up Review of the Inspection Recommendations', April 2021, www.cjini.org/getattachment/48e855ca-cd40-4283-83c2-720cf49b5c94/report.aspx
7 For example, the need for a holistic approach is discussed by Killean R., '"A leap forward"? Critiquing the criminalisation of domestic abuse in Northern Ireland', (2020) 71 *Northern Ireland Legal Quarterly* 595.
8 Discussion of the need for such measures can also be found in McQuigg R.J.A., *International Human Rights Law and Domestic Violence*, 2011, Routledge, Abingdon, at 31–33; and in McQuigg R.J.A., *The Istanbul Convention, Domestic Violence and Human Rights*, 2017, Routledge, Abingdon, at 95–96.
9 Schneider E.M., *Battered Women & Feminist Lawmaking*, 2000, Yale University Press, New Haven, at 52.
10 Randall M., 'Symposium: Domestic violence & the law: Theory, policy, and practice: Domestic violence and the construction of 'ideal victims': Assaulted women's 'image problems' in law', (2004) 23 *Saint Louis University Public Law Review* 107 at 144.
11 Schneider, op. cit., at 196–197.
12 'Covid-19: One year on – A Joint Statement from Women's Aid, Imkaan, Women's Aid Federation Northern Ireland, End Violence Against Women, Welsh Women's Aid and Scottish Women's Aid', 23 March 2021, www.womensaid.org.uk/covid-19-one-year-on/
13 Stanley N., Barter C., Farrelly N., Houghton C., McCabe L., Meinck F., Richardson Foster H. and Shorrock S., 'Innovation, Collaboration and Adaptation: The UK Response to Domestic Abuse under Covid-19', December 2021, DAHLIA-19, University of Central Lancashire and University of Edinburgh, at 23.
14 Women's Research and Development Agency, 'Women's Aid Launch a Petition for a Violence Against Women and Girls Strategy in NI', 9 March 2021, https://wrda.net/2021/03/09/womens-aid-launch-a-petition-for-a-violence-against-women-and-girls-strategy-in-ni/
15 Department of Health, Department of Justice and Executive Office, 'Call for Views – New Strategies', 10 January 2022, https://consultations.nidirect.gov.uk/doj/call-for-views-dsa-strategy-vawg-strategy-response/, at 18.

Bibliography

Aldridge J., '"Not an either/or situation": The minimization of violence against women in United Kingdom "domestic abuse" policy' (2021) 27 *Violence Against Women* 1823.

Armatta J., 'Getting beyond the law's complicity in intimate violence against women' (1997) 33 *Willamette Law Review* 774.

Barnett A., '"Like gold dust these days": Domestic violence fact-finding hearings in child contact cases' (2015) 23 *Feminist Legal Studies* 47.

Berry D.B., *The Domestic Violence Sourcebook*, 1998, Lowell House, Los Angeles.

Bettinson V., 'Criminalising coercive control in domestic violence cases: Should Scotland follow the path of England and Wales?' (2016) Criminal Law Review 165.

Bettinson V., 'Aligning partial defences to murder with the offence of coercive or controlling behaviour' (2019) 83 *Journal of Criminal Law* 71.

Bettinson V. and Bishop C., 'Is the creation of a discrete offence of coercive control necessary to combat domestic violence?' (2015) 66 *Northern Ireland Legal Quarterly* 179.

Bettinson V. and Robson J., 'Prosecuting coercive control: Reforming storytelling in the courtroom' (2020) 12 *Criminal Law Review* 1107.

Bishop C., 'Domestic Violence: The Limitations of a Legal Response', in S. Hilder and V. Bettinson (eds.), *Domestic Violence – Interdisciplinary Perspectives on Protection, Prevention and Intervention*, 2016, Palgrave Macmillan, London, 59–79.

Bishop C. and Bettinson V., 'Evidencing domestic violence, including behaviour that falls under the new offence of "coercive and controlling behaviour"' (2018) 22 *International Journal of Evidence and Proof* 3.

Bruce E., 'Attitudes of Social Workers and Police in the Select Committee Report on Violence to Women and Children', in University of Bradford (ed.), *Battered Women and Abused Children – Intricacies of Legal and Administrative Intervention*, 1979, Issues Publications, University of Bradford, 50–61.

Burman M. and Brooks-Hay O., 'Aligning policy and law? The creation of a domestic abuse offence incorporating coercive control' (2018) 18 *Criminology and Criminal Justice* 67.

Burton M., *Legal Responses to Domestic Violence*, 2008, Routledge-Cavendish, Abingdon.

Burton M., 'The human rights of victims of domestic violence: *Opuz v Turkey*' (2010) 22 *Child and Family Law Quarterly* 131.

Cairns I., 'What counts as "domestic"? Family relationships and the proposed criminalization of domestic abuse in Scotland' (2017) 21 *Edinburgh Law Review* 262.

Cairns I., 'The *Moorov* doctrine and coercive control: Proving a "course of behaviour" under s.1 of the Domestic Abuse (Scotland) Act 2018' (2020) 24 *International Journal of Evidence and Proof* 396.

Connelly C. and Cavanagh K., 'Domestic abuse, civil protection orders and the "new criminologies": Is there any value in engaging with the law?' (2007) 15 *Feminist Legal Studies* 259.

Cook R.J., 'Women's International Human Rights Law: The Way Forward', in R.J. Cook (ed.), *Human Rights of Women – National and International Perspectives*, 1994, University of Pennsylvania Press, Pennsylvania, 3–36.

Cretney A. and Davis G., 'Prosecuting 'domestic' assault' (1996) Criminal Law Review 162.

Cretney A. and Davis G., 'Prosecuting domestic assault: Victims failing courts, or courts failing victims?' (1997) 36 *The Howard Journal* 146.

Diduck A. and Kaganas F., *Family Law, Gender and the State*, 1999, Hart Publishing, Oxford.

Dobash R.P. and Dobash R.E., 'Women's violence to men in intimate relationships: Working on a puzzle' (2004) 44 *British Journal of Criminology* 324.

Douglas H., 'Do we need a specific domestic violence offence?' (2015) 39 *Melbourne University Law Review* 434.

Douglas H. and Fitzgerald R., 'Strangulation, domestic violence and the legal response' (2014) 26 *Sydney Law Review* 231.

Doyle J.L. and McWilliams M., 'Intimate Partner Violence in Conflict and Post-Conflict Societies', May 2018, Political Settlements Research Programme, Edinburgh.

Doyle J.L. and McWilliams M., 'What difference does peace make? Intimate partner violence and violent conflict in Northern Ireland' (2020) 26 *Violence Against Women* 139.

Duggan M. and Grace J., 'Assessing vulnerabilities in the Domestic Violence Disclosure Scheme' (2018) 30 *Child and Family Law Quarterly* 145.

Edwards S., 'New Directions in Prosecution', in J. Taylor-Browne (ed.), *What Works in Reducing Domestic Violence? A Comprehensive Guide for Professionals,* 2001, Whiting & Birch Ltd, London, 211–238.

Edwards S., 'The strangulation of female partners' (2015) 12 *Criminal Law Review* 949.

Ellison L., 'Prosecuting domestic violence without victim participation' (2002) 65 *Modern Law Review* 834.

Evason E., *Hidden Violence: A Study of Battered Women in Northern Ireland*, 1982, Farset Co-op Press, Belfast.

Fitz-gibbon K., Walklate S. and McCulloch J., 'Editorial introduction' (2018) 18 *Criminology and Criminal Justice* 3.

Forbes E.E., 'The Domestic Abuse (Scotland) Act 2018: The whole story?' (2018) 22 *Edinburgh Law Review* 406.

Fredman S., *Human Rights Transformed – Positive Rights and Positive Duties*, 2009, Oxford University Press, Oxford.

Freedman A.E., 'Symposium: Fact-finding in civil domestic violence cases: Secondary traumatic stress and the need for compassionate witnesses' (2003) 11 *American University Journal of Gender, Social Policy & the Law* 567.

Goodmark L., 'Symposium: Domestic violence & the law: Theory, policy, and practice: Law is the answer? Do we know that for sure?: Questioning the efficacy of legal interventions for battered women' (2004) 23 *Saint Louis University Public Law Review* 7.

Grace J., 'Clare's Law, or the national Domestic Violence Disclosure Scheme: The contested legalities of criminality information sharing' (2015) 79 *Journal of Criminal Law* 36.

Hague G. and Malos E., *Domestic Violence: Action for Change*, 2005, New Clarion Press, Cheltenham.

Hague G., Mullender A., Aris R. and Dear W., 'Abused Women's Perspectives: Responsiveness and Accountability of Domestic Violence and Inter-Agency Initiatives', 2001, Report to the ESRC.

Hall M., 'The relationship between victims and prosecutors: Defending victims' rights?' (2010) Criminal Law Review 31.

Hanmer J. and Griffiths S., 'Effective Policing', in J. Taylor-Browne (ed.), *What Works in Reducing Domestic Violence? A Comprehensive Guide for Professionals,* 2001, Whiting & Birch Ltd, London, 123–150.

Hanna C., 'The paradox of progress: Translating Evan Stark's coercive control into legal doctrine for abused women' (2009) 15 *Violence Against Women* 1458.

Herring J., *Domestic Abuse and Human Rights*, 2020, Intersentia, Cambridge.

Hesselbacher L., 'State obligations regarding domestic violence: The European Court of Human Rights, due diligence, and international legal minimums of protection' (2010) 8 *Northwestern Journal of International Human Rights* 190.

Hester M., Hanmer J., Coulson S., Morahan M. and Razak A, *Domestic Violence: Making it Through the Criminal Justice System,* 2003, University of Sunderland and Northern Rock Foundation, Sunderland.

Hester M. and Westmarland N., 'Tackling Domestic Violence: Effective Interventions and Approaches', Home Office Research Study 290, 2005, Home Office Research, Development and Statistics Directorate.Hirschl R., '"Negative" rights vs. "positive" entitlements: A comparative study of judicial interpretations of rights in an emerging neo-liberal economic order' (2000) 22 *Human Rights Quarterly* 1060.

Hughes B., 'Can domestic violence be considered a violation of human rights law?' (2006) 14 *British Journal of Midwifery* 192.

Hughes M., 'The Domestic Abuse (Scotland) Act 2018: A general guide and civil ramifications' (2019) 20 *Scots Law Times* 59.
Humphreys C. and Thiara R.K., 'Neither justice nor protection: Women's experiences of post-separation violence' (2003) 25 *Journal of Social Welfare and Family Law* 195.
James A., 'In practice: Prosecuting domestic violence' (2008) *Family Law* 456.
Jeffries S., 'In the best interests of the abuser: Coercive control, child custody proceedings and the "expert" assessments that guide judicial determinations' (2016) 5 *Laws* 14.
Johnson M.P., 'Conflict and control: Gender symmetry and asymmetry in domestic violence' (2006) 12 *Violence Against Women* 1003.
Killean R., '"A leap forward"? Critiquing the criminalisation of domestic abuse in Northern Ireland' (2020) 71 *Northern Ireland Legal Quarterly* 595.
Kimmel M.S., '"Gender symmetry" in domestic violence: A substantive and methodological research review' (2002) 6 *Violence Against Women* 1332.
Kuennen T.L, 'Analysing the impact of coercion on domestic violence victims: How much is too much?' (2007) 22 *Berkeley Journal of Gender, Law and Justice* 2.
Lacey N., *Unspeakable Subjects*, 1998, Hart Publishing, Oxford.
Lewis R., 'Making justice work: Effective legal interventions for domestic violence' (2004) 44 *British Journal of Criminology*, 204.
Martin L., 'Debates of Difference: Male Victims of Domestic Violence and Abuse', in S. Hilder and V. Bettinson (eds.), *Domestic Violence – Interdisciplinary Perspectives on Protection, Prevention and Intervention*, 2016, Palgrave Macmillan, London, 181–201.
McGorrery P. and McMahon M., 'Criminalising "the worst" part: Operationalising the offence of coercive control in England and Wales' (2019) 11 *Criminal Law Review* 957.
McMahon M. and McGorrery P. (eds.) *Criminalising Coercive Control: Family Violence and the Criminal Law*, 2020, Springer, Singapore.
McQuigg R.J.A., *International Human Rights Law and Domestic Violence*, 2011, Routledge, Abingdon.
McQuigg R.J.A., 'A contextual analysis of the Council of Europe's Convention on Preventing and Combating Violence Against Women' (2012) 1 *International Human Rights Law Review* 367.
McQuigg R.J.A., 'What potential does the Council of Europe Convention on Violence Against Women hold as regards domestic violence?' (2012) 16 *International Journal of Human Rights* 947.
McQuigg R.J.A., 'Gender Based Violence and the Legal Perspective: An International Overview', in K. Nakray (ed.), *Gender-based Violence and Public Health*, 2013, Routledge, Abingdon, 40–53.
McQuigg R.J.A., 'The European Court of Human Rights and Domestic Violence: *Valiuliene v Lithuania*' (2014) 18 *International Journal of Human Rights* 756.
McQuigg R.J.A., 'Domestic violence as a human rights issue: *Rumor v Italy*' (2015) 26 *European Journal of International Law* 1009.

McQuigg R.J.A., 'The CEDAW Committee and gender-based violence against women: General Recommendation No 35' (2017) 6 *International Human Rights Law Review* 263.

McQuigg R.J.A., *The Istanbul Convention, Domestic Violence and Human Rights*, 2017, Routledge, Abingdon.

McQuigg R.J.A., '*Kurt v Austria*: Applying the *Osman* test to cases of domestic violence' (2020) *European Human Rights Law Review* 394.

McQuigg R.J.A., '*Kurt v Austria*: Domestic violence before the Grand Chamber of the European Court of Human Rights' (2021) European Human Rights Law Review 550.

McQuigg R.J.A., 'Northern Ireland new offence of domestic abuse' (2021) *Statute Law Review*, early online access: https://doi.org/10.1093/slr/hmab013

McQuigg R.J.A. 'The European Court of Human Rights and Domestic Violence: *Volodina v. Russia*' (2021) 10 International Human Rights Law Review 155.

McWilliams M. and McKiernan J., *Bringing It Out in the Open: Domestic Violence in Northern Ireland*, 1993, HMSO, Belfast.

McWilliams M. and Ní Aoláin F., '"There is a war going on you know": Addressing the complexity of violence against women in conflicted and post conflict societies' (2013) 1 *Transitional Justice Review* 4.

Merry S.E., 'Rights talk and the experience of law: Implementing women's human rights to protection from violence' (2003) 25 *Human Rights Quarterly* 343.

Meyersfeld B., *Domestic Violence and International Law*, 2010, Hart Publishing, Oxford.

Miles J., 'Domestic Violence', in J. Herring (ed.), *Family Law – Issues, Debates, Policy*, 2001, Willan Publishing, Devon, 78–124.

Mills O., 'Effects of domestic violence on children' (2008) *Family Law* 165.

Mullender A. and Hague G., 'Women Survivors' Views', in J. Taylor-Browne J (ed.), *What Works in Reducing Domestic Violence? A Comprehensive Guide for Professionals,* 2001, Whiting & Birch Ltd, London, 1–33.

Nakray K. (ed), *Gender-based Violence and Public Health*, 2013, Routledge, Abingdon.

Randall M., 'Symposium: Domestic violence & the law: Theory, policy, and practice: Domestic violence and the construction of 'ideal victims': Assaulted women's 'image problems' in law' (2004) 23 *Saint Louis University Public Law Review* 107.

Robinson A. and Cook D., 'Understanding victim retraction in cases of domestic violence: Specialist courts, government policy, and victim-centred justice' (2006) 9 *Contemporary Justice Review* 189.

Schneider E.M., *Battered Women & Feminist Lawmaking*, 2000, Yale University Press, New Haven.

Smith L.J.F., 'Domestic Violence: An Overview of the Literature', 1989, Home Office Research Study 107, HMSO, London.

Stanko E.A, *Intimate Intrusions*, 1985, Routledge, Abingdon.

Stanley N., Barter C., Farrelly N., Houghton C., McCabe L., Meinck F., Richardson Foster H. and Shorrock S., 'Innovation, Collaboration and Adaptation: The UK Response to Domestic Abuse under Covid-19', December 2021, DAHLIA-19, University of Central Lancashire and University of Edinburgh.

Stark B., 'Symposium on integrating responses to domestic violence' (2001) 47 *Loyola Law Review* 255.

Stark E., *Coercive Control: How Men Trap Women in Personal Life*, 2007, Oxford University Press, Oxford.

Stark E., 'Rethinking coercive control' (2009) 15 *Violence Against Women* 1509.

Stark E., 'Looking beyond domestic violence: Policing coercive control' (2012) 12 *Journal of Police Crisis Negotiations* 199.

Stark E. and Hester M., 'Coercive control: Update and review' (2019) 25 *Violence Against Women* 81.

Sullivan C.M., 'Using the ESID Model to reduce intimate male violence against women' (2003) 32 *American Journal of Community Psychology* 295.

Tadros V., 'The Distinctiveness of Domestic Abuse: A Freedom Based Account' in A. Duff and S. Green (eds.), *Defining Crimes*, 2005, Oxford University Press, Oxford, 119–142.

Thomas C., 'Domestic Violence', in K.D. Askin and D.M. Koenig (eds.), *Women and International Human Rights Law* (Vol.1), 1999, Transnational Publishers Inc, New York, 219–256.

Tolmie J.R., 'Coercive control: To criminalize or not to criminalize?' (2018) 18 *Criminology and Criminal Justice* 50.

Tuerkheimer D., 'Recognising and remedying the harm of battering: A call to criminalise domestic violence' (2004) 94 *Journal of Criminal Law and Criminology* 959.

Williamson E., 'Living in the world of the domestic violence perpetrator: Negotiating the unreality of coercive control' (2010) 16 *Violence Against Women* 1412.

Youngs J., 'Domestic violence and the criminal law: Reconceptualising reform' (2015) 79 *Journal of Criminal Law* 55.

Index

For Product Safety Concerns and Information please contact our EU representative GPSR@taylorandfrancis.com
Taylor & Francis Verlag GmbH, Kaufingerstraße 24, 80331 München, Germany

www.ingramcontent.com/pod-product-compliance
Ingram Content Group UK Ltd.
Pitfield, Milton Keynes, MK11 3LW, UK
UKHW021245190926
475569UK00001BA/7
9781032199658